Vintage Craft Workshop

FRESH TAKES ON TWENTY-FOUR CLASSIC PROJECTS FROM THE '60S AND '70S

Cathy Callahan

Photographs by Meiko Takechi Arquillos

Text copyright © 2011 by Cathy Callahan.

Photographs copyright © 2011 by Meiko Takechi Arquillos.

Library of Congress Cataloging-in-Publication Data:

Callahan, Cathy.
    Vintage craft workshop : fresh takes on twenty-four classic projects from the '60s and '70s / Cathy Callahan.
        p. cm.
    Includes bibliographical references and index.
    ISBN 978-0-8118-7532-5 (pbk.)
    1. Handicraft. I. Title.

TT157.C2154 2011
745.5—dc22

2010023637

Manufactured in China
Designed by Emily Craig

10 9 8 7 6 5 4 3 2 1

Chronicle Books LLC
680 Second Street
San Francisco, California 94107
www.chroniclebooks.com

This book is dedicated to Fran.

Contents

Introduction

"Nothing is new, but personal interpretation can often be so."

Alexander Girard, 1956

Where it all started for me. (Cover of Dip Film Flowers *by James E. Gick, 1968.)*

My obsession with crafts from the '60s and '70s stems from my childhood. I was raised by a super-crafty mom in suburban Southern California, and I was completely surrounded by the do-it-yourself craft aesthetics of the time. To live in my house was to experience a never-ending process of making—with a constant whirlwind of craft supplies and projects in various stages of completion. As soon as I was old enough to start making my own crafts, my mom allowed me to choose some supplies of my own from a local craft store. I had been fascinated with their in-store samples of intensely colored plastic flowers. They were made by twisting wire into the shape of petals, which were then dipped into a liquid plastic and allowed to dry. The individual petals were grouped together to create a flower. The product I needed was something called "dip film," and I chose hot pink. Within a few days, my bedroom was decorated with my new creations. Sadly, you can't buy dip film anymore—or maybe that's a good thing, since it was not exactly environmentally friendly—but the memory of making those flowers has stuck with me. That's where it all started for me.

My collecting habits started as a teenager, when I realized that a treasure trove of great vintage stuff was to be found at thrift stores and flea markets for next to nothing. Later, the Internet aided and intensified my collecting—I have to admit that I went totally nuts once eBay came along. For me, though, it's not just about finding something old and placing it on a shelf to admire. I love to explore the history of the object and to find out more about the person who designed it or the company that manufactured it.

Almost everything I have done to earn a living has involved the making of or arranging of things. In my work as a window dresser, I make props for shop windows. Window displays are ephemeral, though, and I have always found it frustrating when the installation is over and the props are often thrown out. I wanted to make things with a little more permanence, so a few years ago, on a lark, I applied for the Bazaar Bizarre craft show in San Francisco. To my great surprise I was accepted—even though I didn't have any products or any idea of what it was that I was going to sell!

I made a few things and asked some friends what they thought, and one of them told me they looked "very Hazel Kaboodle." Hazel who? She explained that Hazel Kaboodle was the woman who made the craft kits that her family used when she was growing up. I had never heard of her. An eBay search revealed that my friend's recollection was a little off. "Hazel Kaboodle" was actually a woman named Hazel Pearson who wrote and published how-to books and distributed craft supplies, and "Kaboodles" was what she called her craft kits. An eBay auction for a book by Hazel called *Make It with . . . Yarn 'n Burlap* caught my eye, so I placed a bid and ended up winning the auction. Little did I know that the book I was about to receive would lead me to a huge discovery and down an entirely new path.

When the book arrived and I flipped through the pages, I realized—and yes, it was one of those "moments" that they talk about on daytime TV—that these were the same kind of things my mom made. I don't remember her having any how-to books, so the sort of craft techniques in these books must have been shared informally among crafters like my mom at that time. As it turns out, Hazel was an important innovator and tastemaker in the world of crafts, and she played a key role in popularizing the kinds of crafts my mom did. She founded her own craft-supply company in a Los Angeles suburb in the late 1940s, as an independent businesswoman heading her own company at a time when that was very much the exception to the rule. I realized there was much more to this craft world than I could have imagined, and I began to accumulate vintage craft books at an ever-increasing rate.

As I started to participate in more craft shows, I found my growing collection of vintage craft books to be an indispensable source for ideas and inspiration— and they were really fun to look at, too. I wanted to share the inspiration I was getting from those books, so I decided to start a blog (www.cathyofcalifornia. typepad.com). It wasn't too long before the blog started to get comments from other people who love vintage crafts as much as I do.

Through craft shows and blogging, I began to meet some very talented people. I started wondering what would happen if I asked some of these contemporary artists and crafters to reinterpret projects from the vintage craft books that I find so inspiring. Well, this book is the answer to that question.

A few years ago, a reader of my blog sent me a vintage flower loom and at first I wasn't really too sure what to do with it, but I played around with it and made a few flowers. One thing led to another, and before I knew it I was on national television making flowers with Martha Stewart on her show! During the segment, she said that we were "taking something old and making it very new again." Martha's words get right to the heart of this book, since in one way or another, all of the contributors have created their projects with this notion in mind. Each of the projects is inspired by a craft technique from the '60s and '70s, but they have been executed in ways that make them fresh and new. My favorite part of putting this book together was seeing the different ways the contributors approached vintage craft projects, and the surprising ways in which they brought them into the present. I selected the artists based on their particular areas of expertise, matching them with the projects from my vintage craft books that I thought best suited their talents. Some were introduced to crafts or techniques that were new to them, while others updated old favorites, but they all embraced the process of rediscovering and reinterpreting something from the past.

Each project includes step-by-step instructions and, in some cases, a picture of the original vintage project that inspired the new one as well as a photo of the crafter's completed project. The projects in this book do not require any special skills or expensive tools and, if you make things on a regular basis, it's likely that you already have everything you need. If not, a quick visit to a local craft, sewing, or art-supply store or an online source should be all that's needed to get you up and running. For the most part we have specified the use of new materials, but if you can get your hands on vintage supplies and tools, then all the better.

I am so happy that the contributors to this book have found inspiration from vintage crafts just as I have, and I hope you will too.

Crafty Innovators of the '60s and '70s

Some of my fondest memories are of accompanying my mom on shopping trips to the local craft store just a few blocks from our home in suburban San Diego. This would have been in the late 1960s or early 1970s. The shop was independently owned and run by a couple that my mom was friendly with. They no doubt kept my mom informed about all the latest products and project ideas. I remember being fascinated by all of the craft supplies on the shelves, and the possibilities they promised.

Our neighborhood craft shop was just one of hundreds that sprouted up across the country in the years following the Second World War. Americans found themselves with more leisure time, and many began to take up hobbies such as leather crafting, model airplane building, and paint-by-numbers. Demand grew for the special tools and supplies that were required for these various interests. Recognizing an opportunity, creative entrepreneurs began to start companies that specialized in manufacturing and distributing everything that was needed for this new and widespread pursuit of leisure.

The business world of the time was dominated by men, and this burgeoning craft and hobby industry was no exception, but in the late '40s and early '50s, a few independent-minded women started their own craft supply companies—many based in Southern California, surprisingly close to where I lived. They, too, created specialized products, and they sometimes even repurposed products intended for other uses, such as Styrofoam, which could be used to make handicrafts (a term that became widely used in the postwar period to describe popular crafts, as opposed to fine crafts or folk arts). These women popularized supplies that brought new options to home crafters, including wood fiber for sculpting flowers, resin for casting home décor items, and foam shapes for arranging festive centerpieces. They also introduced a whole new genre of craft how-to books for instruction and inspiration.

As these craft-supply businesses grew in the '60s and '70s, the women who ran them became regarded as experts. They enjoyed a measure of fame and had very loyal followings. The craft industry was driven by novelty to a certain extent, though, and they had to keep dreaming up new ideas for products to keep their businesses going.

Aleene Jackson: Not So Tacky Trailblazer

Practically every craft project my mom ever made involved the use of Aleene's Tacky Glue in some way, and whenever I see one of those gold plastic bottles, it reminds me of her. You can still buy it today and it really is good stuff. It bonds materials together quite well and dries clear.

When I began finding craft books from the '60s and '70s, a few books from Aleene's Craft "How-To" Create series made their way into my collection. I fell in love with the projects I found in her books, and I was fascinated to discover that Aleene was an actual person—not a Betty Crocker-like corporate persona—who ran her own company based in suburban Los Angeles. It's a safe bet that the neighborhood craft shop my mom frequented was fully stocked with Aleene's products, including her most famous invention, Tacky Glue.

Aleene Jackson is one of those forward-thinking women who started her craft business in the '40s, opening retail and wholesale stores, teaching classes, and appearing on television when it was an exciting and untested new medium. Her influence expanded in the '50s and '60s through her products and promotional verve. In 1968, she took to the road on the Craft Caravan—her visionary cross-country road show that traveled to thirty-three cities promoting craft supplies. The first stop was in Pasadena, California, where fifteen thousand people showed up and the line was three blocks long just to get in!

Here's Aleene at her store in Temple City, California, in the late '60s. On the shelves behind her you can see many of her products, including her famous Tacky Glue.

What intrigues me most about Aleene is the way she started her business. She opened a floral shop in Arcadia, California, in 1944, and though her shop was reasonably successful she saw that many of her customers were looking for something more. They were creative and resourceful, and she realized they had the potential to do their own arrangements and save a little money if only they had access to professional supplies. She started selling these supplies (floral wire, tape, ribbon, foam, etc.) so her customers could make centerpieces and corsages with their homegrown flowers. Soon business was booming and she had orders from all over California because no one else was retailing floral supplies at the time. It turned out that there was a reason no one else was doing this. In what could be seen as a measure of her success, florists felt their business was being threatened, and the California Floral Association attempted to prevent her from purchasing supplies wholesale. She sued them and won the right to continue her business, and she moved forward from there with a revived sense of possibility. Her willingness to challenge the status quo and her entrepreneurial spirit helped to define the world of popular crafts. I honestly believe that craft supplies and craft-supply stores as we know them today would not exist if it weren't for her.

Chapter 1:
Make It with Burlap . . . and a Little Felt

I love burlap for its coarse texture. Typically made from jute, it was originally intended for use as a backing for hand-stitched rugs. It became an iconic craft material in the '60s and '70s—look at any craft book from the time and you will likely see burlap used in some way. It's inexpensive, it's easy to work with, and it can be used in all sorts of interesting ways. The most popular color is probably natural, but it's also available in a wide range of hues.

Cover of Hazel Pearson's Make It with . . . Yarn 'n Burlap, *1969.*

Burlap Tips

1. The dyes used to color burlap can sometimes run, so if you are using glue or Mod Podge to adhere burlap to a surface, it's a good idea to do a little test first.

2. Some burlap is loosely woven, so you might have to double your fabric if you are covering a surface that might show through. Or you may paint the surface in a matching color.

3. It's best to use heavy-duty shears when cutting burlap.

4. Burlap can also be painted. Experiment using your favorite craft paint.

5. It's easy to fringe burlap by pulling out lengthwise threads along the edge.

A Note on Styrofoam

Styrofoam has long been used as a structural material in crafts. Aleene Jackson had a central role in popularizing it: While sourcing floral supplies for her first store, she met a salesman who had samples of the then-new product, a war-surplus material that was developed for its buoyancy. Seeing the potential for its use in crafts, she purchased some and showed it to her father. He designed some equipment for her that allowed her to create foam shapes (such as eggs) for crafts. Pre-formed Styrofoam shapes went on to become a staple of craft-supply stores. Today's environmental concerns cause many to think twice before using foam products—and rightly so. Luckily, for craft projects (such as the Mushroom Pincushion in this chapter), it is used in small quantities and the resulting objects have long and useful lives.

Hazel (at far left) about to head
out on the Craft Caravan.

CRAFTY
LADY

Hazel Pearson:
Queen of Kaboodle

From Shasta Daisies to Mod Monster Animals, the classic craft book *Make It with . . . Yarn 'n Burlap* is loaded with ideas. It's one of possibly hundreds of books from the Handicrafts for Fun Library published by Hazel Pearson. I love that just about every project from the book is featured on the cover.

Based in Rosemead, California, Hazel was a real powerhouse in the world of handicrafts. She first made her mark in crafts in the late '40s by popularizing copper tooling, a technique in which a design is traced on thin copper and made dimensional using special tools. Hazel designed the patterns, wrote instruction

books, and sold supplies and kits, and she would go on to do the same for a wide range of other craft techniques. In addition to teaching and publishing how-to books, she developed a full line of craft supplies that were distributed nationwide, including her famous "Kaboodles" craft kits (as in "the whole kit and . . . "). As promised on the packaging, her kits included "everything you need to create something beautiful" for projects such as string art, latch hook pillows, and straw flowers.

Even though Hazel and Aleene Jackson were competitors, they were also friends and they still are to this day. Hazel played a big role in Aleene's Craft Caravan.

Mushroom Pincushion

by Susan Beal

In the '60s and '70s, mushrooms seemed to pop up everywhere in crafts. One of my favorite mushroom-inspired crafts is this pincushion I found in Hazel Pearson's *Burlap Bounty*. I reworked the project and sold my version at an early Felt Club craft fair. Susan purchased one from me and uses it every day in her sewing room, so I asked her to create her own version for this book. I love that she chose a two-tone color palette.

TOOLS

→ Serrated knife (an old steak knife works well)
→ Measuring tape
→ Drafting compass
→ Pencil
→ Fabric scissors
→ Paper scissors
→ Stem template (see templates)
→ Straight pins
→ One 1-in/2.5-cm-wide foam brush
→ Mod Podge
→ Aleene's Tacky Glue
→ Hot glue gun and glue stick

MATERIALS

→ One 5-in/12.5-cm white Styrofoam ball
→ One 9-x-4-in/23-x-10-cm white Styrofoam cone
→ Two 9-in/23-cm squares burlap, in complementary colors
→ Wool felt:
   One 12-in/30.5-cm square, for bases
   Three 4-in/10-cm squares, in complementary colors, for flowers
→ 26 in/66 cm ½-in/12-mm trim
→ Toothpicks

INSTRUCTIONS

1. Use the serrated knife to cut the Styrofoam ball in half as you would a grapefruit (set one half aside to make another pincushion later, if you like). Next, cut off 2½ in x 6 cm from the top and bottom of the Styrofoam cone, leaving a 4-in/9-cm-tall middle piece.

2. Use the compass to trace a 9-in/23-cm circle on the burlap color that you wish to use for the cap of the mushroom, and cut the circle out with scissors. Cut out the Stem template, trace the shape on the second square of burlap, and cut it out.

3. From the 12-inch/30.5-cm felt square, use the compass to measure one 5-in/12.5-cm and one 2½-in/6-cm circle (for bases), and cut them out.

TIP: Styrofoam pieces can vary in size, so err on the side of generosity when trimming the burlap and felt to fit your pieces.

4. Center the burlap circle over the top of the Styrofoam ball half, and hold it in place with a straight pin. Make small folds around the perimeter of the circle to gather up the extra material, using pins to secure it. It's easiest to make one fold, secure it, and make a second one directly across the circle after that. Rotate around the circle, making a total of 8 small folds that are fairly symmetrical. Trim away extra fabric below the bottom edge of the Styrofoam.

5. Use scissors to cut a 1½-in/4-cm X in the center of the 5-in/12.5-cm felt circle, and press the piece to the underside of the cap. Using your fingertips or thumb, press through the X, into the center of the cap underside, creating a small recess. Remove the felt from the cap.

6. Use the foam brush to spread an even coat of Mod Podge on the underside of the cap and the base of the stem. Tack down the felt circles of corresponding size. Smooth the felt with your fingers to make sure it's secure.

7. Secure the burlap folds all around the mushroom cap with small dabs of hot glue. (Be careful not to put much hot glue directly on the Styrofoam or it will melt.) Hold each fold together while the glue cools, removing the pins as you go.

8. Add a thin line of glue around the perimeter of the cap, over the raw edges and folds. Add 16 in/40.5 cm of the trim over the glue, using a straight pin to hold one end in place, and bring the trim all the way around the circle. Secure both raw edges with pins, and cut excess trim away neatly.

9. Use the foam brush to apply a layer of Mod Podge to the cone, and wrap the burlap stem covering around it, leaving at least half an inch of extra fabric at the top, and making sure the vertical edge of the burlap is neat. Trim away extra fabric at the bottom if any extends past the Styrofoam edge. Add a little extra Tacky Glue to secure the straight vertical edge of the burlap. Add 8 in/20 cm of trim around the bottom of the stem the same way you added it to the cap in step 8.

10. Gather the extra material at the top of the cone and pierce it with 3 toothpicks, leaving an inch or so sticking up. Add a generous dab of Tacky Glue inside the cap's recess and then push the mushroom's stem inside the cap; the toothpicks will hold it in place neatly. (Note: Make sure the trim's overlap areas are not exactly lined up on the cap and stem; it's better to have them at different places.)

11. Using the compass, trace one 2-in/5-cm circle (for flowers) and one ¾-in/2-cm circle (for centers) on each of the 4-in felt squares, and cut them out. Snip 6 tiny V shapes in each flower to create "petals." Glue the centers on the flowers, and then glue the flowers to the area where trim overlaps on the mushroom cap.

SUSAN BEAL is a writer and crafter and is the author of *Bead Simple, Button It Up,* and *The World of Geekcraft.* She writes about things she likes and projects to make at Westcoastcrafty.com. She lives in Portland, Oregon.

Flower Wastepaper Basket

by Cathy Callahan

I remember my mom making wastepaper baskets like these when I was a girl. She would go to the neighborhood Baskin-Robbins ice cream store and ask if she could have the leftover ice cream buckets when they were empty. She would then cover them in burlap and decorate them with bits of felt, yarn, or whatever else suited her fancy. Much to my delight, I found a picture of a very similar project in the pages of Hazel Pearson's *Burlap Bounty* (1967).

Baskin-Robbins no longer gives their used buckets away, unfortunately. I asked at the neighborhood store, and I'm pretty sure they thought I was crazy. As an alternative, I substituted a plastic trash can I found at The Container Store. A cylindrical form works best to enhance your applied decoration.

And you don't have to use it just as a wastepaper basket. It also makes a great umbrella stand or addition to craft room for storing stuff like bolts of fabric or rulers.

→ Measuring tape
→ Fabric scissors
→ Mod Podge
→ One 2-in/5-cm-wide foam brush,
→ Paper scissors
→ Flower Wastepaper Basket templates (see templates)
→ Pencil
→ Aleene's Tacky Glue
→ Toothpicks
→ Tweezers (optional)

MATERIALS

→ 1 cylindrical wastepaper basket (Mine was 14 in/35.5 cm tall and 10 in/25 cm in diameter.)
→ ¾ yd/68.5 cm burlap, for the exterior (more or less, depending on the size of your wastepaper basket)
→ ¾ yd/68.5 cm burlap, in a complementary color, for the interior (more or less depending on the size of your wastepaper basket)
→ Three 14-x-10-in/35.5-x-25-cm pieces wool felt, in complementary colors, for flowers
→ Three 1½-yd/137-cm lengths 2-mm jute twine (or yarn), in complementary colors, for flowers

P.S.

This same technique for applying burlap to a surface can be used on other items—picture frames, boxes, journals, and what have you.

INSTRUCTIONS

1. Measure the exterior and interior circumference and height of the wastepaper basket.

2. From the burlap for the exterior, cut a piece ¼ in/6 mm shorter than the height and ½ in/12 mm longer than the circumference of the basket. From the burlap for the interior, cut a piece 1 in/2.5 cm taller than the height and ¼ in/6 mm shorter than the circumference. As a "trial run," place the burlap on the outside and inside of the can in the manner it will be applied to double-check your measurements. Adjust as needed.

3. Using the foam brush, apply an even coat of Mod Podge to the interior of the basket. Carefully apply the interior color burlap. Smooth it with your hands to flatten out creases and air bubbles. Apply a line of Mod Podge along the top of the exterior, and wrap the excess burlap from the interior around the lip and smooth out with fingers.

4. You will want to consider where your joins are. I suggest that the exterior join be directly across from the interior. When viewed from the front of the basket, the join in the exterior will be on the back of the basket and the interior join in the front inside.

5. Brush an even coat of Mod Podge on the exterior of the basket. Carefully apply the exterior color burlap. Smooth out with your hands to flatten out creases and air bubbles. You will notice that the exterior color ends just shy of the top, exposing just a little color from the interior.

6. Using a copier or scanner, enlarge the flower and 2 center-shape templates by 143%. Print, cut out the templates, and trace the shapes onto your felt. Next, cut each element out of each color of felt. (If your wastepaper basket is larger or smaller than the one used here, use a scanner or copier to reduce or enlarge the templates as needed or desired.) Arrange as shown in the photo, gluing each set of flower pieces together.

7. Cut an 18-in/46-cm length of each color of twine, twirl into a spiral shape (referring to photo), and glue to the center of each flower.

8. Cut ten ¾-in/2-cm snips of each color twine for the petal details and glue them down (again referring to photo for placement). Toothpicks and tweezers can be of help when applying these tiny details. Cut a 9-in/23-cm length of each color twine for the stems, and three 2½-in/6-cm lengths of each color for the leaves. Glue the twine to the flowers.

9. Spread an even layer of glue to the back of each flower and apply it to the wastepaper basket. Make sure that the design is placed on the "front" and that the exterior join faces the "back."

Birdhouse String Dispenser

by Jenny Ryan

In addition to all the independently published craft books of the '60s and '70s, some of the many popular women's magazines of the day would also feature craft projects. Of these, my favorite is *McCall's Needlework & Crafts*, though *Better Homes and Gardens* is a close second.

I saw these cute string dispensers in a *McCall's Needlework & Crafts* made using old plastic bleach bottles. I thought it was a good idea to use recycled bottles, but who really uses bleach anymore? Jenny Ryan came up with the perfect idea for a substitution and used a cardboard oatmeal canister instead.

- → Two 1-in foam brushes: 1 for paint, 1 for glue
- → X-Acto knife
- → Measuring tape
- → Fabric scissors
- → Sobo Craft & Fabric Glue
- → Dessert plate or saucer, to use as a template
- → Drafting compass
- → Birdhouse String Dispenser templates (see templates)
- → Clothespins or paper clips
- → Straight pins
- → Sewing needle
- → Embroidery needle
- → ¼-in/6-mm hole punch

MATERIALS

- → Empty oatmeal canister (Jenny used the 18-oz/510-g Quaker Oats brand.)
- → FolkArt Acrylic Paint to match burlap, to coat canister interior and cardboard scraps
- → ½ yd/46 cm burlap
- → Cardboard scraps (Old cereal boxes work great.)
- → Wool felt scraps in various colors
- → Patterned cotton fabric scraps, in 2 or 3 various prints
- → Thread to match fabric
- → Small handful bamboo fiberfill, to stuff bird
- → Small metal jump ring (big enough for string to fit through)
- → Embroidery floss, for bird's talons
- → Small twig or dowel, approximately 5 in/12.5 cm long
- → 1 yd/91.5 cm rickrack trim
- → 3 or 4 small glass beads per flower, or as desired

P.S.

Reuse the discarded oatmeal canister lid by using it as a palette for your craft paint.

Because we use recycled cardboard scraps in this project, you'll need to cover the markings with craft paint so they don't show through the burlap's open weave. If you'd like to eliminate this step, use colored cardboard that matches the burlap.

Add additional embellishments using millinery trims, flowers, sequins, or ribbons.

INSTRUCTIONS

1. Remove the lid from the oatmeal canister and wipe down the inside. Cover the outside with craft paint using a foam brush, and let it dry. Using an X-Acto knife, cut a 1-in/5-cm hole on one side of the canister, approximately 3 in/10 cm up from the base.

2. Cut out a 9-x-13-in/23-x-33-cm piece of burlap. Apply fabric glue to one side using a foam brush. Center the oatmeal canister along one short edge of burlap and roll until the burlap covers the canister; let it dry. Once dry, use scissors to trim away excess burlap at the top and bottom of the canister. Using the X-Acto knife, cut into the excess burlap covering the hole you cut in step 1. Fold the burlap inside the hole, and glue it in place to hide the raw edges.

3. Cut a small circle from a scrap of cardboard using a dessert plate or saucer as a tracing template. The circle should be 1 in/2.5 cm or so larger than the diameter of the oatmeal canister. If using recycled packaging, cover any printing with craft paint and let dry.

4. Cut out 1 felt circle and 1 burlap circle using the same template you used in step 3. Using a foam brush, cover the painted side of the cardboard circle with fabric glue and smooth the burlap over it. Next, cover the other side of the circle with fabric glue and smooth the felt over it. Set aside to dry.

5. Use the compass to trace and cut out a 9½-in/24-cm circle from cardboard. Cut away one quarter of the circle (think of it as pie that you are cutting). If using recycled packaging, cover any printing with craft paint and let dry. Trace the same-size circles (with the quarter cut away) and cut them out from 1 piece of burlap and 1 piece of cotton. When the paint is dry, cover the painted side of the cardboard with fabric glue and smooth the burlap over it. Next, cover the other side of the cardboard with fabric glue and smooth the cotton over it. Squeeze fabric glue along 1 short edge of the roof piece, and roll it, with the burlap facing out, into a cone shape. Hold the cone in place with clothespins or paper clips, and set it aside to dry.

6. Cut out the Birdhouse String Dispenser template pieces. From the patterned fabric, trace the Underside template and cut it out. From a different piece of patterned fabric, trace the Body template and cut it out. Flip over the Body template to get the mirror image of the piece just cut, trace it onto your third patterned fabric, and cut it out. Pin the Body pieces right sides together, and sew from the beak to tail using a simple whipstitch. Attach the Underside by placing the right sides together and sewing from head to tail, one side at a time. Leave a 1-in/2.5-cm hole along one side and turn the bird right-side out. Stuff it with bamboo fiberfill and sew the opening closed. Attach a metal jump ring to the bird's beak, using a needle and thread to secure it.

7. Using embroidery floss and a needle, affix the bird to the twig. Use 3 to 4 stitches on either side of the bird's base to mimic the look of talons. For added strength, squeeze a thin line of fabric glue between the bird and twig and let dry.

8. Using the X-Acto knife, poke a small hole into the oatmeal canister about ¼ in/6 mm beneath the larger hole created in Step 1. This hole should be smaller than the diameter of the twig. Push the end of twig into the hole so that ½ in/12 mm pokes through to the inside. Cut 4 to 5 small circles from felt, and punch a hole in the center of each. Dab the circles with fabric glue and slide them onto the twig from inside the canister. Add more circles until the twig seems fully supported and let dry.

9. Squeeze a thin line of fabric glue around the underside of the canister and center it on the burlap circle from step 4. Cut a length of rickrack to cover the outer edge of the burlap circle and glue it into place; set aside to dry.

10. Cut a length of rickrack to cover the roof's edge, and glue it into place; set aside to dry.

11. Using scrap fabrics, wool felt, and glass beads, cut out and stitch together some small, simple flowers and leaf shapes and glue them onto the birdhouse where desired. To give the flowers some dimension, cut out petal shapes, pinch the centers, and stitch them in place to form a pleat. Create 4 to 6 petals and stitch them together at the centers to create a flower.

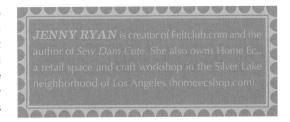

JENNY RYAN is creator of Feltclub.com and the author of *Sew Darn Cute*. She also owns Home Ec., a retail space and craft workshop in the Silver Lake neighborhood of Los Angeles (homeecshop.com).

Gone Fishing Tote

by Kayte Terry

This image comes from the collection of Charles Phoenix, who collects vintage Kodachrome slides from the '40s through the '60s, and shares his discoveries in his books and live performances. Most of the photos in his collection are family slides found at garage sales and thrift stores. I love old family photos; they are a fascinating window into the way people used to live—the home décor, the food, and of course the crafts.

When I showed Kayte Terry this photo, she fell in love with the tote the lady with the poodle is holding. It looks just like one I saw pictured in a *McCall's Needlework & Crafts* and I'd wager that this lady made the bag herself from the pattern in that magazine. Kayte wanted to add her own little twist to the project, so she made the bag a bit smaller than the original and replaced the hanging fish with appliqués using scraps of Liberty print and wool felt. It's the perfect mash-up of ladylike, retro, and preppy.

- Gone Fishing Tote patterns and templates (see templates)
- Tracing paper
- Pencil
- Paper scissors
- Straight pins
- Quilting mat and ruler
- Tailor's chalk
- Fabric scissors
- Sobo Craft & Fabric Glue
- Embroidery needle
- Sewing machine
- Iron
- Sharpie permanent marker
- Towel or press cloth

MATERIALS

- ¼ yd/23 cm burlap, for Bag Top
- ¼ yd/23 cm burlap, in complementary color, for Bag Bottom
- 2 skeins embroidery floss
- Thread, in matching and contrasting colors
- ½ yard/46 cm cotton fabric, for lining
- 1 sheet double-stick fusible webbing (ultra heat bond)
- Scraps of fabric, for fish appliqués
- Scraps of felt, for fish appliqués

INSTRUCTIONS

1. Use a photocopier to enlarge the Gone Fishing Tote patterns and templates by 286%. Each square on the grid, once enlarged and copied, should be 1 in/2.5 cm. Transfer the enlarged patterns and templates to tracing paper and then cut them out using paper scissors.

2. Pin the Bag Top pattern to the burlap in the color you have selected for the top of your bag. Cut out the pattern piece from the burlap. Repeat this step to get a second Bag Top piece. Pin the Bag Bottom pattern to the burlap in your second color, then cut it out. Repeat this step to get a second Bag Bottom piece.

3. Set 1 of the Bag Tops right-side up on a quilting mat. Using a quilting ruler and tailor's chalk, mark lines at a 45-degree angle every 1 in/2.5 cm across the entire piece. Then mark lines at a 45-degree angle every 1 in/2.5 cm in the other direction.

4. Cut pieces of embroidery floss and place them over each of the chalk lines on the bag top, in both directions. Affix the ends of each piece of the embroidery floss to the bag with a dot of fabric glue.

5. Thread a needle with embroidery floss, knotted at the end. Make 1 stitch over the spot where each of the diagonal floss lines intersect, and knot each one on the back of the Bag Top. This will secure your "fishnet" in place.

6. Pin 1 Top and 1 Bottom burlap piece together, right sides facing. Using a sewing machine, sew them together (use a denim needle if desired) leaving a ½-in/12-mm seam allowance. Repeat for the remaining Top and Bottom burlap pieces. Using the high setting on your iron, press the seams open.

7. Use 1 sewn burlap piece as a template for the lining of the bag: Fold the lining fabric in half, and pin the sewn burlap piece to the fabric. Trim around the edges of the burlap piece, cutting through both layers of fabric to create 2 lining pieces.

8. With a Sharpie, trace the fish templates and details onto the paper side of 1 sheet of double-stick fusible webbing. Cut roughly around each pattern piece.

9. Choose which fabrics and felt pieces you want to use for the parts of the fish. Peel off the side of the fusible webbing that you didn't trace on, and fuse it to the wrong side of your chosen fabric or felt according to the manufacturer's instructions. Cut out each fish detail.

10. Lay out the front of the bag right-side up on a clean surface (protect your surface with a towel or press cloth) and lay out your fish and details according to the photo or follow your own design. Peel off the backing of the fusible webbing and fuse the fish and details to the bag front according to the manufacturer's instructions.

11. Using a contrasting thread and a straight stitch, sew around each fish and fish detail, backstitching at the beginning and the end to secure. Trim any excess threads.

12. Place the front and back of the bag with right sides together, and pin. Sew along the sides, bottom, and top of the bag, leaving a ½-in/12-mm seam allowance. Do not sew along the curved edges. Repeat step 12 with the lining pieces from step 7.

13. Trim seams and clip corners with the tips of scissors, then turn the bag right-side out. Repeat step 13 for the lining.

14. With tailor's chalk, mark a curved line ½ in/12 mm from the edge of the curve of the handles on the outside of the bag. With scissors, clip along the curve to the marked line (this makes it easier to turn the fabric) and turn the edges ½ in/12 mm to the wrong side. Press. Repeat step 14 with the lining but press the raw edge ½ in/12 mm to the right side.

15. Insert the lining into the bag, wrong sides together, and slip stitch the curved edges of the lining to the outside of the bag. Topstitch all around the curved handles, ½ in/ 12 mm in from the edge.

KAYTE TERRY is a stylist, crafter, and the author of *Complete Embellishing* and *Appliqué Your Way*. She lives in Philadelphia with her husband and her rabbit and muse, Potato. To find out more about what Kayte's up to, check out her blog: Thisisloveforever.com.

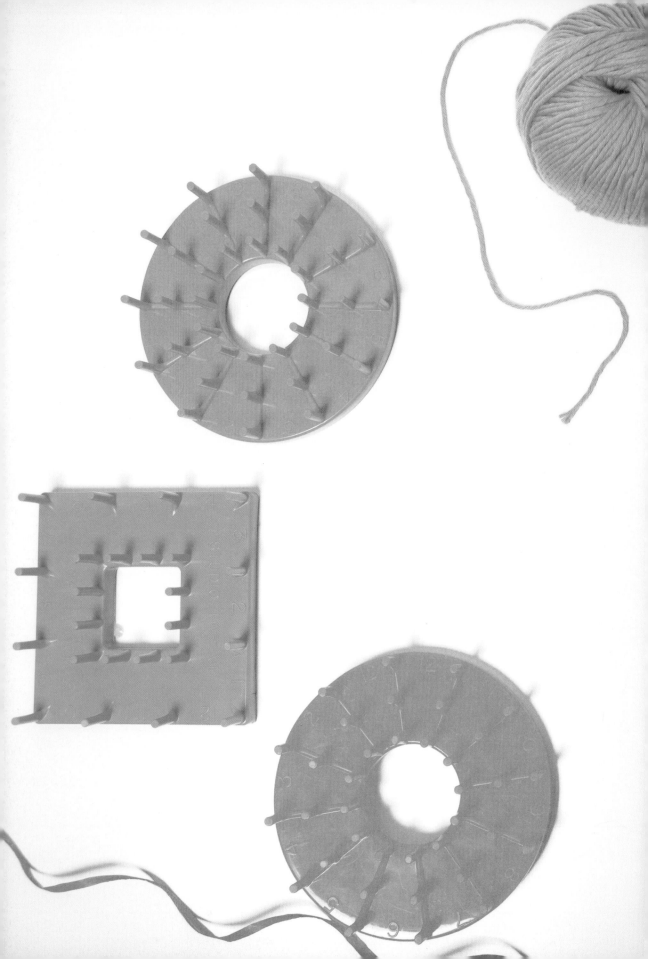

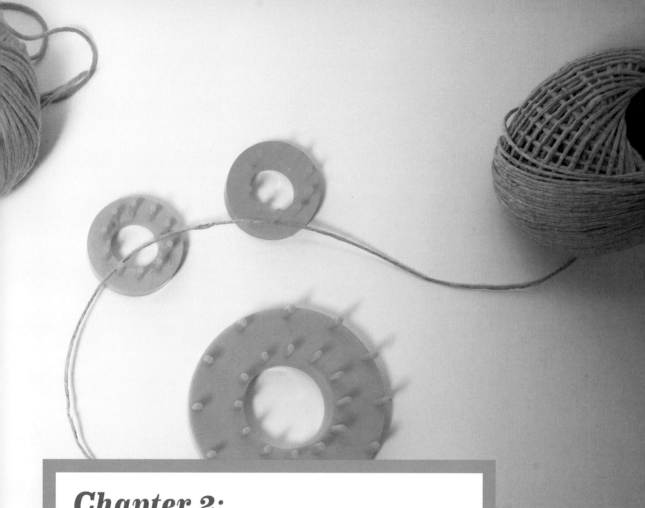

Chapter 2:
Ideas for
Raffia 'n' Yarn

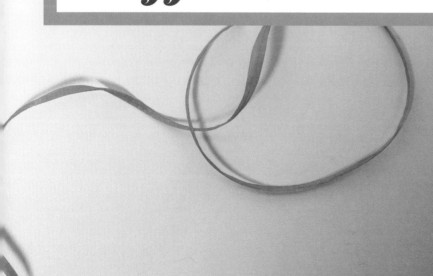

Raffia and yarn can be used interchangeably in many craft projects. I love yarn, but raffia appeals to me on an entirely different level. I think my passion for raffia began when I first laid my eyes on *Swistraw and Flower Looms* by LeJeune Whitney from 1972—my favorite craft book of all time.

Raffia Tips

In the '60s and '70s, raffia for use in crafts was sold under a variety of different brand names, and old stock of LeJeune's Swistraw, Hazel Pearson's Ribbon Straw, Bucilla's Strawtex, and Columbia-Minerva's HiStraw can still be found today although it is becoming increasingly rare. It typically came in 24-yd skeins. I think the textures and colors of vintage raffia are better than what's currently available, but new raffia works just as well. Raffia is now sold primarily for wrapping gifts and is available in 60-ft or 100-yd rolls. I suggest using synthetic (rayon) raffia for craft projects because I have found that paper raffia tears too easily and natural raffia has too many slubs. Raffia is available in both a shiny (sometimes referred to as "pearlized") and a matte finish.

Flower Loom Tips

Flower looms are small, round (and sometimes square) plastic shapes with a series of pegs. You wrap the material of your choice (yarn, raffia, string, ribbon, thread, or even wire) around the pegs in a figure-eight formation. There are many variations in how it can be done, and many ways of layering shapes and colors. Once you've created a flower, the center is stitched using a tapestry needle in order to hold the flower together before you pop it off the loom.

Some looms have stationary pegs and others are adjustable. There is also the Knit Wit, a little device with retractable metal pegs. All of these work well, but my go-to loom is my trusty vintage Studio Twelve Magni-Fleur.

There are many ways loomed flowers can be used for home décor or on clothing and accessories. I like to attach them to floral wires and pop them in a vase, or attach a pin-back to make a brooch.

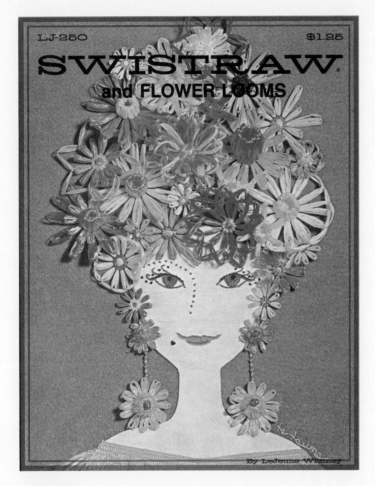

LJ-250

SWISTRAW.
and FLOWER LOOMS

$1.25

By LeJeune Whitney

//

Cover of Swistraw and Flower Looms
by LeJeune Whitney, 1972.

CRAFTY
LADY

LeJeune Whitney:
Craft Sophisticate

LeJeune Whitney was based in Sunnyvale, California. She was quite the entrepreneur and launched many successful businesses, and in the late '60s and early '70s she focused her talents on crafts. In addition to designing and manufacturing craft supplies, she also published many books, including *Macramé—A New Look at an Ancient Art* and *Crocheting with Swistraw*. LeJeune not only wrote all of her books but she was also responsible for the design and photography, and there's something about her books that suggests a more sophisticated aesthetic than that of her peers. I get the feeling that she was aware of fine-craft publications like *Craft Horizons* and drew ideas and inspiration from the worlds of fine arts and professional design. I think she aspired to a higher level and saw the connections between fine craft and the popular handicrafts of the day.

Loomed Flower Wall Hanging

by Cathy Callahan

LeJeune Whitney designed and created most of the projects that appear in her books, and her imaginative wall hangings are probably my favorite. Here's my version, which combines my love of both vintage crafts and contemporary Japanese craft supplies. The flower loom I used is from Japan, as is the fabric I used for the backing. The leaves were stitched using *sashiko* (a style of Japanese embroidery) thread.

TOOLS

- Measuring tape
- Fabric scissors
- Iron and ironing board
- Handheld staple gun
- $5/16$-in/8-mm staples
- Clover Hana-Ami Flower Loom (instructions and needle are included with the loom)
- Ruler
- Pencil or fabric marker
- Aleene's Tacky Glue
- Toothpicks
- Embroidery needle

MATERIALS

- 1 yd/91.5 cm home decorating weight fabric (I used Echino Solids by Etsuko Furuya in mustard.)
- One 18-x-24-x-1½-in/46-x-61-x-4-cm gallery panel (cradled with a plywood frame)
- One 60-ft/18.5-m spool raffia, in matte chocolate, for flower petals
- One 60-ft/18.5-m spool raffia, in matte black, for flower petals
- One 60-ft/18.5-m spool raffia, in matte ivory, for flower petals
- 20 yd/18.5 m $1/32$-in/1-mm natural jute twine or yarn, in brown, for flower centers
- 20 yd/18.5 m $1/32$-in/1-mm natural jute twine or yarn, in black, for flower centers
- 20 yd/18.5 m $1/32$-in/1-mm natural jute twine or yarn, in natural, for flower centers
- 3 yd/2.5 m $3/8$-in/1-cm ribbon, in black, for flower stems
- 3 yd/2.5 m $3/8$-in/1-cm ribbon, in brown, for flower stems
- Scraps of wool felt, in brown, black, and natural, for leaves
- Embroidery floss, in brown, black, and natural, for leaves (I used Japanese *sashiko* thread.)

INSTRUCTIONS

1. Measure and cut the fabric into a 23-x-29-in/58.5-x-73.5-cm rectangle. Iron out all wrinkles. Lay the fabric out, and center the gallery panel (face down) on top of it. You should have 2½ in/6 cm extra on all sides. Wrap the fabric around to the back of the panel, and staple it in place to the frame. Keep fabric taut and even as you go.

TIP: There will be excess fabric at each corner. Fold fabric in the same manner that you would handle the corners when wrapping a gift, and then staple them down.

2. Follow instructions for the loom and make 3 single-layer large flowers, 3 single-layer medium flowers, and 3 double-layer (large and medium combined) flowers. Please refer to photo of completed project for colors of the petals (in raffia) and the colors for the center (in jute or yarn). All flowers are finished using the basic darning stitch.

TIP: Don't worry if you can't get your hands on a vintage flower loom (which of course you can use if you have one). Clover's "Hana-Ami" Flower Loom from Japan is now being imported into the United States and is readily available. It is fun and simple to use.

3. Lay the completed flowers on the fabric-covered board and arrange as shown on photo of completed project. You will want to have the stems (the thin ribbon) spaced evenly, so measure accordingly and draw a pencil line where each stem will be placed. Starting from the center and measuring out, I spaced the stems 2¼ in/5.5 cm apart.

4. Cut ribbon to size for each stem. Carefully run a very thin bead of glue down each pencil line and apply the ribbon, making sure you keep a clean line. Clean up any excess glue with a toothpick.

5. Glue the flowers in place.

6. Cut leaf shapes from the felt. Use embroidery floss and a needle to do a quick running stitch down the center of each leaf. Glue to secure the leaves in place.

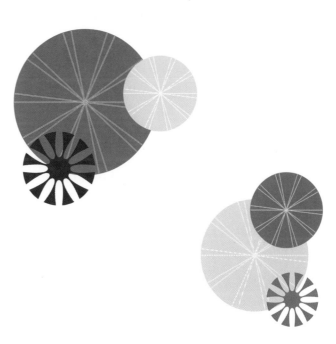

Mod Circle Place Mats

by Diane Gilleland

Diane's inspiration: Photo-graph from the cover of Serendipity in HiStraw, *1970.*

Plastic canvas for needlepoint doesn't get much respect in the craft world, but it's a material with tremendous possibilities. No one is working harder today to explore the untapped potential of plastic canvas and to raise its profile than Diane Gilleland. Her projects avoid all of the clichés one would normally expect from the technique, so I knew that she was the right person to create a project inspired by *Serendipity in HiStraw* (1970).

You probably think of yarn when you think of plastic canvas, but for this project, Diane used a mixture of both new and vintage raffia. Don't worry if you've never tried needlepoint before—the two stitches used here are very easy to master.

- ➤ Scissors
- ➤ Measuring tape
- ➤ Tapestry needle, size 13
- ➤ Chenille needle, size 18
- ➤ Blue painter's masking tape
- ➤ Aleene's Tacky Glue

MATERIALS

(PER PLACE MAT)

- ➤ One 13½-x-10½-in/34-x-26.5-cm sheet 7-count plastic canvas
- ➤ Eight 4¼-in/11 cm plastic canvas rounds (See Tip.)
- ➤ One 100-yd/91.5-m spool synthetic raffia, for panels (Diane used the pearlized gold color.)
- ➤ Two 24-yd/22-m skeins vintage Swistraw, in contrasting colors, for circles
- ➤ 2 yd/1.8 m 24-lb. test fishing line

P.S.

Plastic canvas rounds come in various sizes. The 4¼-in/11-cm-diameter rounds used here are vintage, and can be found through sources like www.eBay.com and www.Etsy.com. You can also adapt the design to accommodate the more readily available 3- or 5-in-/7.5- or 12.5-cm-diameter rounds.

INSTRUCTIONS

1. Using scissors, cut the sheet of plastic canvas into 3 pieces: one 6¼-x-10½-in/16-x-26.5-cm center section, and two 1½–x-10½-in/4-x-26.5-cm side sections.

In the spaces between these sections, you'll need to fit 4 or more plastic canvas rounds. There should be a half round at the top and bottom for stability, with additional rounds fitted side-by-side between them. The rounds should be sized so they touch end to end. Trim your rounds as needed.

2. Using the tapestry needle, stitch the center and side panels with the raffia, using the zigzag stitch (see facing page).

3. Using Swistraw, stitch each plastic canvas round using the continental stitch (see facing page). Start at the outermost row and work toward the center. The design pictured was stitched with 4 outer rows in 1 color and the center rows in a contrasting color. Stitch around the edges of all pieces with an overcast stitch (see facing page).

4. Lay the finished pieces out on your work surface, right-side up, arranging them in the configuration of the finished place mat. Thread the chenille needle with approximately 8 in/20 cm of fishing line, but don't tie a knot in it. Begin with 1 of the half rounds. At the point where this round contacts the bottom of the center panel, make 2 or 3 stitches to connect the panels. Tie the ends of the fishing line in a double knot at the back. Don't trim the ends of the fishing line away yet.

5. Repeat this process to connect the other side of this half round to the side section. Repeat steps 4 and 5 to connect another half round to the top of the place mat.

6. Fit the full rounds into the space between the half rounds. Tape them in place with the painter's tape so they won't move around when you're stitching. Repeat steps 4 and 5 to attach the sides of each round to the center and side panels. Knot the ends of the fishing line together at the back of the place mat as you go.

7. Last, make 2 or 3 stitches at the point where each pair of rounds touches. Tie the fishing line in a double knot at the back.

8. Flip the place mat over. Put a small drop of glue over every fishing line knot. Allow the glue to dry.

9. Trim away all the excess ends of fishing line.

10. Repeat steps 4 to 9 to add the second column of rounds.

TIP: When stitching on plastic canvas, it's best not to tie knots in your raffia or Swistraw. To begin a strand, bring your needle up through the canvas, leaving about a 2-in/5-cm tail at the back. Then, catch this tail in the backs of your stitches.

TIP: To end a strand, pass the needle under a few stitches at the back of the work and cut away the excess. If you're having trouble finding a spot to pass your needle under, you can just glue the end of the strand to the back of the work with craft glue.

DIANE GILLELAND is a craft writer, designer, and publisher. She produces CraftyPod.com, a blog and podcast about making stuff, has published numerous e-books for crafters, and is the author of *Kanzashi in Bloom*. She lives in Portland, Oregon.

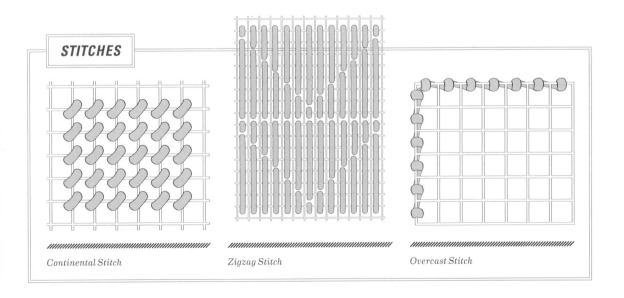

STITCHES

Continental Stitch

Zigzag Stitch

Overcast Stitch

Free-Form Crochet Vase Covers

by Cecily Keim

I can't crochet to save my life, but I just love this bottle-cozy project from *Crocheting with Swistraw* (1972) by LeJeune Whitney, so I turned to Cecily Keim, who has been crocheting since the age of nine. She, too, saw the possibilities in this project and was excited to try it out. Instead of using bottles, we decided to use vases from Heath Ceramics, which suit the technique perfectly.

Cecily did a few tests using raffia and we were not happy with the results—they felt "cold" against the vases. The use of three colors just didn't feel right either. She switched to a single color of yarn and then it all just clicked.

TOOLS

- ➔ 1 crochet hook, size F (3.75 mm) (for small vase cozy base)
- ➔ 1 crochet hook, size F/5 (4.0 mm) (for small vase cozy body)
- ➔ 1 crochet hook, size G/7 (4.5 mm) (for larger vase cozy base)
- ➔ 1 crochet hook, size H (5.0 mm) (for larger vase cozy body)

MATERIALS

- ➔ One 136-yd/125-m skein Patons Grace yarn (100 percent cotton)

CROCHET STITCHES USED
(AND ABBREVIATIONS)

- ➔ chain: ch
- ➔ slip stitch: sl st
- ➔ single crochet: sc
- ➔ double crochet: dc

P.S.

You may choose to use a different yarn; in that case simply use the hook appropriate for the job. Each cozy was made with 2 different hook sizes, 1 to crochet the base and 1 to crochet the body.

A Note from Cecily

The instructions for the inspiration piece simply said to crochet a base and go from there, so I did. The important thing is to take this inspiration and the elements described here to create your own piece of crocheted art. Inspiration from the original piece by LeJeune Whitney set me to work and I found myself making up my own way to crochet a cozy. Figuring it out and crocheting without a set pattern were the real joys of the project!

For more ideas about stitch patterns to try or help with increases and decreases, check out *Teach Yourself Visually Crocheting*.

The following techniques and stitch combinations were used to build the free-form cozies:

Increase: 2 stitches worked into 1 stitch.

Decrease: Skip a stitch or work 2 stitches together (see a crochet how-to for this).

Hole: Work chain stitches, then skip over 1 or more stitches from the previous round and stitch into the next stitch from the previous round to create a hole. In the next round, work stitches into the chain stitches to shape the hole. Holes are a great way to warp an even-looking area and create rows that have interesting waves.

Shell: Work 4 or 5 double crochet stitches into 1 space. (You can refer to *Teach Yourself Visually Crocheting* for how to make a shell stitch.) Play around with this combination to create different shells; try working taller stitches or add a chain between the stitches.

Crunchy Texture: Single crochet in next stitch, chain 1, skip the next stitch, repeat to the end of the round. In the following round, work single crochet into the chain spaces, chain 1, and skip the single crochets. To add more uneven "crunch" and waves to a round, try throwing in taller stitches such as half double, double, or triple crochet stitches.

Cozy Base

Make a ring of chain stitches that fits the base of the vase. Slip stitch the last chain to the first chain to finish the ring.

Round 1: Work the first round of sc stitches into the ring. Use enough stitches to fill the ring.

Round 2: Work 2 sc into the first sc of the first round and 1 sc into the next sc of the previous round. Work 2 sc into the next sc and 1 sc into the next sc, repeat this pattern to finish the second round. Sl st to the first stitch to join.

Round 3: Work 2 sc into the first sc of the first round and 1 sc into each of the next 2 sc of the previous round. Work 2 sc into the next sc and 1 sc into each of the next 2 sc. Repeat this pattern to finish the third round. Sl st to the first stitch to join.

Round 4: Work 2 sc into the first sc of the first round and 1 sc into each of the next 3 sc of the previous round. Work 2 sc into the next sc and 1 sc into each of the next 3 sc. Repeat this pattern to finish the fourth round. Sl st to the first stitch to join.

Continue to work rounds with gradual increases until the cozy base is the same size as the vase base. Use as many or as few rounds as you need. There is no right or wrong way, as long as the base fits your vase. When you are ready to start the body of the cozy: Work rounds of even stitches or, if needed, add increases or decreases as necessary to fit the shape of your vase. Now you're ready for the fun part—free-forming your own unique cozy. Here is an explanation for how these 2 cozies were made:

Small Vase

The small vase cozy was made using rounds of single crochet and holes to change the shape of the rounds. Crochet the base using the smaller F (3.75 mm) hook and switch to the larger F/5 (4.0 mm) hook for the body of the cozy.

To add interest to the hole spaces, try working a shell combination in a hole or in the corner next to one. This provides a nice contrast to the neat single crochet texture and can also be used to shape the cozy. If you use holes and shells, you'll find your rounds don't look like normal even rounds, but start to take on a wave-like look instead.

Once the cozy is partially done, you may wish to work with the cozy on the vase. Set yourself free to follow your whim, working different elements to shape the cozy. Use increases, decreases, holes, and shells to sculpt the cozy.

Larger Vase

For the larger vase, use a G/7 (4.5 mm) crochet hook for the base and an H (5.0 mm) hook for the body). Using a larger hook creates a more open netted look. The stitch combination for this cozy uses alternating single crochet and chain stitches. This creates a "crunchy" texture that adjusts well to increases, decreases, and any other element you may choose to use in building and shaping your cozy.

Once you've made your base, work rounds of the "crunchy texture" pattern. Shells and holes were used for this vase too. Work with the cozy on the vase to shape it just the way you want it.

> TIP: As you build and shape the cozy, you may find you've reached a dead end. Extend the loop on the hook over the neck of the vase. Either tie off this loop or continue without cutting the yarn: Stretch the attached yarn to the next space you'd like to work into, use a slip stitch to fasten, and continue working. These loops of yarn become a different element in the design and can be used to tighten and shape the cozy. This works best on a vase or bottle with a neck that can hold the loops in place. A wide-mouthed vase won't hold the loops as well.

An art teacher's daughter, **CECILY KEIM** grew up experimenting with her mother's art supplies and still loves trying out new tools, techniques, crafts, and—best of all—making fabric. She is the author of *Teach Yourself Visually Crocheting*. Find more of her work at Suchsweethands.com.

Crocheted Mobile

by Laura Normandin

I have admired Laura Normandin's delicate crochet work for a long time. Her style suggested a perfect approach to rethinking this late-'60s crocheted wall panel that I spotted in *McCall's Annual of Creative Handcrafts*. We both loved the colors and textures of the original, but Laura was inspired to use natural wool in a subtler color palette. She also went a step further and decided to make it a mobile, giving it some movement and layering.

For this mobile, Laura crocheted 19 discs and hung them from some wood strips cut down to size. To make the discs, she used variations on a simple pattern of crocheting in the round. It's quite fun to add colors and variation to the round doilies once you get the hang of it!

Crocheted discs

- 1 crochet hook, size 9 (1.40 mm) or similar

MATERIALS

- 1 spool pearl cotton thread, size 8
- 1 skein each lace- and weaving-weight yarns
- 1 spool linen string

CROCHET STITCHES USED
(AND ABBREVIATIONS)

- chain: ch
- slip stitch: sl st
- single crochet: sc
- double crochet: dc
- chain-# space: ch-1 sp (number of chains can vary)

To make the mobile

TOOLS

- Iron with steam setting
- Small handsaw (such as X-Acto X75300 Precision Razor Saw Set)
- Sandpaper
- Miter box (optional)
- 1 crochet hook, size 11 (1.10 mm)
- Super Glue

MATERIALS

- Fabric spray starch
- 19 crocheted discs
- One 2-ft-/61-cm-long ½-x-¼-in/12-x-6-mm wood strip
- 1 spool of cotton thread, size 50 or similar

P.S.

I'm not sure that the manner in which Laura crocheted the discs would lend itself to the use of raffia, but if you are experienced in crochet, you might want to experiment with raffia to create similar discs.

Crocheted discs

INSTRUCTIONS

Variation 1

Round 1: Ch 4, sl st in the 1st ch to form a ring. Ch 3, 14 dc into the ring, sl st into the 3rd ch of the original ch-3 to join the round. Ch 2, turn.

Round 2: 1 dc into same st as turning ch, ch 1, *2 dc in the next stitch, ch 1, repeat from * to end of round. Sl st into the 2nd ch of the original ch-2 to join the round; cut the string and pull the tail through the last stitch.

Round 3: Turn, join new color and begin working in a ch-1 sp from previous row, ch 1, sc in same space, *ch 2, 2 sc in next ch-1 sp, repeat from * to end of round, ending with a ch 2, sl st in the 2nd ch of the original ch-2 to join the round; cut the string and pull the tail through the last stitch. Weave in loose ends.

Variation 2

Round 1: Ch 4, sl st in the 1st ch to form a ring. Ch 3, 14 dc into the ring, sl st into the 3rd ch of the original ch-3 to join the round. Ch 4, turn.

Round 2: *1 dc in next st, ch 2, repeat from * to end of round. sl st into the 2nd ch of the original ch-2 to join the round, cut the string and pull the tail through the last stitch.

Round 3: Turn, join new color and begin working in a ch-2 sp from previous row, ch 2, dc in same space, *ch 1, 2 dc in next ch-2 sp, repeat from * to end of round, ending with a ch 1, sl st in the 2nd ch of the original ch-2 to join the round; cut the string and pull the tail through the last stitch.

Round 4: Turn, join new color, and begin working in a ch-1 sp from previous row. ch 1, sc in same space, *ch 3, 2 sc in next ch-1 sp, repeat from * to end of round, ending with a ch 3, sl st in the ch of the original ch-1 to join the round. Cut the string and pull the tail through the last stitch. Weave in loose ends and trim ends from previous rounds.

Mobile

1. Steam and lightly starch all discs.

2. Using the handsaw, cut the wood strip to lengths of 5 and 12 in/12.5 and 30.5 cm, and sand the cut ends. It helps to rest each piece of wood on a stool or a table, aligning your cut line with the edge, or use a miter box.

3. Using the crochet hook and cotton thread, and leaving an 8-in/20-cm tail, ch 20, attach a disc with a sl st, cut a generous length of thread (depending on how many discs you are adding), and pull the tail through the last stitch. Attach it to the opposite end of the same disc with a sl st, ch 20, and repeat to attach your desired number of discs. Use a sl st to attach the last disc and weave in the loose thread end. Repeat Step 3 to make the remaining strands.

Mimic the photo of the completed project: 2 strands of 2 discs, and 1 strand each of 4, 5, and 6 discs—or as desired.

4. Using a double knot, tie the short strands to the 5-in/12.5-cm wood strip and also attach a thread to the middle of the wood strip, adjusting for balance and trimming ends. Add a dot of glue to the knots to help hold them in place. Tie the remaining strands and the shorter wood strip to the longer wood strip, trim loose ends, and secure each knot with a dot of Super Glue. For a hanger, tie a piece of thread (length as desired depending on where you intend to hang it) loosely to the center of the longer wood strip; hang the mobile from the thread, adjusting for balance by sliding the thread one way or the other. Once your mobile is balanced, secure the hanger thread with a dot of Super Glue.

LAURA NORMANDIN is the artist and craftsperson behind Wrenhandmade.com. She makes dolls, crocheted items, stuffed animals, hair accessories, and paper items as well as fine art. For eleven years, she lent her expertise to *Martha Stewart Living* as a craft editor, making every kind of craft and holiday decoration imaginable. She lives in Brooklyn, New York.

Chapter 3:
Stitching: Crewelwork, Craft Kits, and Appliqué

//
"Dendiform" Wall Hanging
by Jean Ray Laury, 1978.

CRAFTY
LADY

Jean Ray Laury:
The Art of Appliqué

Appliqué is derived from the French word *appliquer*, which simply means "to apply" and is generally defined as the surface attachment of one material to another, typically by means of sewing and/or embroidery, either by hand or by machine. Jean Ray Laury was one of many fiber artists who employed this technique during the '60s and '70s.

I first became aware of Jean's work when I spotted a beautiful wall hanging in the window of a vintage furniture store as I was driving by. I did a double take and pulled over. Unfortunately it was not for sale but the shopkeeper gave me a little background on Jean, including the fact that she had collaborated with (and was at one time married to) Stan Bitters—a sculptor and ceramicist whom I have long admired. No wonder I was drawn to her work!

One of Jean's first large-scale projects was a quilt she created while working toward her master's degree at Stanford. Her first book was *Appliqué Stitchery* (1966),

and it was followed by many others, including my favorite: *Wood Appliqué* (1973). Jean's design activity has included major architectural commissions in stitchery and mosaic, including "Dendriform," which she created in 1978 for the Nut Tree Restaurant in Vacaville, California. The much-loved and fondly remembered Nut Tree showcased an eclectic mix of handcraft and modernism.

Jean still lives and works in Fresno, California. She has written about working in her home studio, and about how her projects sometimes end up taking over the entire house: "Let your home adjust to your activities rather then adjusting your activities to your home," she says—something I can relate to!

Collecting Vintage Craft Kits

There are kits for many types of crafts, but it seems like the ones that involve stitching are the most popular. Craft kits usually include just about everything you need to complete the project; you might only need to provide scissors and maybe an embroidery hoop and you're good to go. Some even come with a frame so you can display your handiwork when you're done, while others include a zipper, piping, and backing so you can make a pillow.

In the '60s and '70s, the marketplace for popular crafts had expanded to the point that famous crafters, fashion designers, and decorators began creating designs for kits. Vera Neumann (you probably know her as simply "Vera") is best known for her floral patterns on everything from place mats to scarves, and she lent her name and designs to countless kits.

Brooke Hodge is an independent architecture and design curator and writer who lives in Los Angeles. She collects vintage '60s and '70s craft kits with a focus on crewel, embroidery, and latch hooking (fifty kits and counting at the time of this writing). I first became aware of her collection when I read her post "It's a Crewel, Crewel World" in The Moment, the *New York Times Magazine* blog.

One day while scouring eBay for vintage Vera linens, Brooke remembered a Vera crewelwork kit that her mother had bought in 1979. Her mother wanted them to work on it together, and they started it but never finished. A few years ago when Brooke was visiting her mother, she asked about the kit—and since Brooke's mom never throws anything away, she still had it. Brooke then finished the kit and enjoyed it so much that she again turned to eBay in search of more. Her search soon expanded to include estate sales and thrift stores.

Brooke has a very keen eye and focuses on kits featuring flowers, nature scenes, owls, and squirrels. Many of the kits were designed by Erica Wilson. She collects both completed and uncompleted kits, as well as kits that have been started but never finished. I personally love the uncompleted kits because you get to see the original diagrams on the fabric or canvas. Next time you visit your mother, auntie, or grandmother, you should ask if she has any old craft kits stashed away in her closet.

Erica Wilson: Creative Stitcher

One day while flipping through the pages of a vintage *McCall's* magazine, I was stopped in my tracks by a series of articles on "creative stitchers." The work by these women was exquisite and verged on fine art. I became particularly fixated on a photo of Erica Wilson in her home studio. She was sitting on the floor pondering what she was working on, but it was the chair sitting next to her that blew my mind. It was a modern chair designed by her husband, mid-century modernist Vladimir Kagan, and upholstered in a floral fabric, an unusual combination to say the least. A few of the blossoms in the fabric print were embroidered by Erica with bold, chunky stitches in shades much richer than the fabric's own colors.

Erica is credited with reviving interest in crewelwork—a decorative form of embroidery using wool instead of cotton thread—in the early '60s. She has written many books on crewel and embroidery and she even hosted her own PBS series. Erica is very prolific and has created an amazing body of work. She has a shop in Nantucket, and her kits are available through her Web site (please see Resources).

//////////////////////////////////////

Vintage Vera stitchery kit from the collection of Brooke Hodge.

Free-Form Crewel Pillow

by Erika Kern

Erika's Inspiration: Re-embroidered fabric designed and worked by Erica Wilson on a Vladimir Kagan chair from Needleplay *by Erica Wilson, 1972.*

For this project, I really wanted Erika Kern to stitch on some upholstery fabric for a couch, but in the end we decided that a pillow might be more practical. Erika explains how she made her pillow here, but it's really up to you on how you want to do the stitching since it will all depend on your choice of fabric.

In Erica Wilson's writings, she encourages her readers to be creative and "scatter your own blossom designs and add your own colors." In her book *Needleplay* (1975) she urged her readers to "think big" (hence my couch idea). So I say if the mood strikes you and that old couch of yours needs to be reupholstered, then go for it.

- Embroidery hoop, size 10, or 9-x-16-in/23-x-40.5-cm scroll-style stretcher bars
- 1 or more chenille needles, size 18
- Measuring tape
- Scissors
- Iron and ironing board
- Press cloth
- Straight pins
- Sewing machine

MATERIALS

- 1 yd/91.5 cm medium-weight, loose-weave fabric or pre-made pillow sham, in a bold floral pattern
- 10 skeins crewel embroidery wool, in 5 colors (2 skeins of each color)
- Thread
- One 20-in-/50-cm-square pillow form (if using fabric), or 1 form to fit your pre-made pillow sham

INSTRUCTIONS

1. Prep the fabric for embroidery: Cut it slightly larger than needed for the finished cover to allow for any shrinkage or fraying that might happen as you stitch. (For example, cut 23-in-58.5-cm square for a 20-in/50-cm square pillow cover.) If using a pre-made sham, you can stitch it as-is or rip apart the side seams. Disassembling the pillow isn't necessary, but it will make it easier to use the hoop and work the stitches.

2. Figure out which part of the fabric's design you'd like to highlight with stitches. Place the fabric in the hoop or stretcher bars, securing tightly so the fabric is taut but not distorted.

3. Begin stitching. This project has no set pattern and is all about enhancing the existing pattern, so have fun with colors and textures. This is your chance to experiment with crewel and traditional embroidery stitches. Two great resources you may refer to are *The Embroiderer's Handbook*, by Margie Bauer, and Erica Wilson's 1973 *Embroidery Book* (search eBay or Amazon). A search on YouTube.com will also turn up several useful stitching tutorials.

Great stitches to start with include stem stitch, French knots, chain stitch, coral knots, and fishbone stitch. These are especially handy on a pre-made pillow sham, since all of these stitches can be easily worked from the front.

4. Once the stitching is complete, remove the hoop or stretcher bars. Press the fabric with a steam iron, wrong side facing up. Turn the fabric right-side up and press with the iron, using a press cloth to protect the embroidery. Then trim it to 22 x 22 in/56 x 56 cm—this is to allot for fraying or warping during stitching.

5. Construct (or reconstruct) your pillow sham: If using fabric, cut it down to fit your pillow. This project used a 20-in-/50-cm-square pillow form, so the fabric was cut into three pieces: one 22-in/56-cm square for the front, and two 17-x-22-in/43-x-56-cm rectangles for the back to create a simple envelope-style pillow cover. After sewing together the sham, I sewed a ½-in/12-mm border around the sham and accented it with a green chain stitch woven with 2 strands of purple.

6. Take 1 of the rectangles you cut in step 5 and fold 1 long edge over ½ in/12 mm and press flat with the iron. Pin the fold in place and sew, stitching about ¼ in/6 mm in from the folded edge. Repeat with the second rectangle.

7. Lay the 22-in/56-cm square right-side up, then place the rectangles right-sides down on top of the square, with the folded and stitched edges overlapping in the middle. Pin around all edges.

8. Sew around all edges of the pillow with a ⅝-in/1.5-cm seam allowance, backstitching in the corners for strength. Turn the pillow cover right-side out and press the seams flat. Insert your pillow form and enjoy!

TIP: You can use new or vintage fabric for this project. The key is to find a medium-weight fabric with a fairly loose weave and a bold pattern. Thrift stores, estate sales, and the Internet are ideal sources.

TIP: Wondering where to find crewel wool? Many cities have specialty needlework shops where you can find it in a wide array of colors and textures. If you don't have a shop in your town, check online. Crewel wool is thinner than tapestry wool or knitting/crochet yarn and is sold in skeins. You can vary the number of strands used as you stitch to change the look of your work.

TIP: When stitching, a large hoop may be easier to handle than stretcher bars—but the bars allow you to work a larger area of fabric at a time. A scroll bar-style stretcher is preferable if you are working with fabric, while a hoop is best when working with a sham.

Here's a list of the flowers on the pillow pictured and the stitches used (from the top, clockwise):

Multicolor flower: with a purple couched lattice interior; center of French knots using 1 strand of green and 1 strand of turquoise worked together; outlined with alternating lines of green stem stitch and orange chain stitch; and finished with a turquoise chain stitch.

Pink flower: stitched with 3 strands of wool in long and short stitch; accented with purple satin stitch using 2 strands of wool; and a center of French knots using 1 strand of purple and 1 strand of orange worked together.

Purple and blue flower: worked with trellis couching stitched with purple trellis and turquoise couching; outlined with 2 rows of green coral stitch using 2 strands of wool.

Orange and purple starburst flower: purple center in long and short stitch using 2 strands of wool and single-strand satin stitches in orange.

Pink flower: worked with 2-strand buttonhole stitch petals and turquoise turkey work (or Ghiordes knot) center using 2 strands.

Small orange flower: outlined in single-strand orange chain stitch and with a green turkey work center using 2 strands.

Purple flower: worked with 2-strand coral knot fill and pink turkey work center using 2 strands.

Orange flower: worked with fishbone stitch petals and center of French knots using 1 strand of purple and 1 strand of green worked together.

ERIKA KERN has been crafting since she was old enough to hold a needle. She is the sole creative force behind MyImaginaryBoyfriend.com, where she writes about crafts and sells wares inspired by her love of nature and all things vintage. Her work has been featured in *Adorn Magazine, Los Angeles Times,* Design*Sponge, and Boing Boing. She lives in Bakersfield, California, with her dog Grace.

Tulip Apron

by Hannah Kopacz

Crafters have long been inspired by nature, and floral themes are probably the most popular subjects. Using appliqué is a good way to incorporate flower shapes into your work. I ran across these adorable aprons in a copy of *Better Homes and Gardens Gifts to Make Yourself* (1972) that I found at my mom's house. Since tulips are a favorite of Hannah Kopacz, I knew she wouldn't mind taking a break from silk-screening to do some machine appliqué for this project.

TOOLS

+ Apron pattern and Tulip templates (see templates)
+ Measuring tape
+ Paper scissors
+ Straight pins
+ Fabric scissors
+ Sewing machine
+ Iron and ironing board

MATERIALS

+ 1 yd/91.5 cm red fabric
+ ¼ yd/23 cm orange fabric
+ ¼ yd/23 cm pink fabric
+ ⅛ yd/11.5 cm light green fabric
+ ⅛ yd/11.5 cm dark green fabric
+ 1 spool red thread
+ 1 spool orange thread
+ 1 spool pink thread
+ 1 spool green thread
+ 1 yd/91.5 cm ⅝-in/1.5-cm grosgrain ribbon, in green
+ 3 yd/2.5 m ½-in/12-mm double-fold bias tape, in red
+ 4 yd/3.5 m ⅞-in/2.5-cm grosgrain ribbon, in red

P.S.

Sturdy cotton or cotton-blend fabrics work well for this project.

If you are appliquéing a garment, think about adding pockets. Each of those tulips is also a pocket!

INSTRUCTIONS

1. Using a scanner or a printer, enlarge the apron pattern and flower templates by 500%. Each square, once copied, should be 5 in/12.7 cm. Cut out the pieces, pin them to your fabrics, and cut around the edges. Remove pins.

2. Place the Tulip Facings and tulip shapes right-sides together and pin. Stitch along the top of the tulips, using a ³/₁₆-in/5-mm seam allowance. Clip the inner corners of each tulip's peaks with the tip of your scissors and turn the tulips right-side out. Press flat with the iron. Topstitch the peaked edge of each tulip using a contrasting shade of thread (see step 3).

3. Using the photo as a placement guide, pin the tulips in place on the apron, then pin on the green grosgrain ribbon stems, with ½ in/12 mm of ribbon tucked beneath the tulip pocket. Using your sewing machine's zigzag stitch, sew each tulip pocket along the sides and bottom, removing the pins as you go, and leaving the peaked tops open. For a punch of color, use a contrasting thread: pink on the orange tulip and orange on the pink tulips. Once the pockets are securely attached, sew down the green stems using matching thread.

4. Using the photo as a placement guide, pin the leaf shapes onto the apron and sew them in place using your machine's zigzag stitch.

5. Pin and sew the bias tape around all raw edges of the apron.

6. Cut the red grosgrain ribbon into four 1-yd/91.5-cm lengths. Starting with 1 length of ribbon, fold the short edge over ½ in/12 mm, and pin it to 1 of the top corners of the apron, sandwiching the raw edge between the ribbon and the back of the apron. Sew in place. If a little extra stability is desired, please refer to the diagram and stitch a rectangle with and X in the middle at any stress points.

Repeat with the remaining lengths of ribbon, pinning and sewing 1 to the other top corner and 1 each to the 2 side corners.

HANNAH KOPACZ is the owner, designer, printer, and seamstress behind Made with Love by Hannah, a clothing company based in Los Angeles, California. Her lifelong love of knickknacks, folk-lore, fairytales, and all manner of vintage cuteness is evident in her designs and her blog, Knick Knacks & Ric Rac (Madewithlovebyhannah.com), in which she catalogs thrift-store finds, fun crafty projects, and endless sources of inspiration. She has been featured in *Bust, Venus,* and *Elle* magazines.

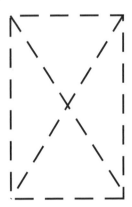

TIP: If you've never sewn with bias tape before, it can be a bit challenging, as you're sewing through several layers of fabric while trying to keep your corners nice and smooth. There are several helpful tutorials on YouTube.com that may help illustrate the process further.

Citrus Slice Bulletin Board

by Nicole Vasbinder

Along with flowers, fruit themes have always been a big favorite in popular crafts. Being California girls, Nicole and I loved the idea of using citrus shapes in her project. Nicole is an amazing seamstress and teacher, but she decided to abandon her sewing machine for this project. Inspired here by the bold fruit themes of the '70s, Nicole hand-appliquéd the citrus slices.

A few tips: While this is a bulletin board, it can also function as a wall hanging. Also, try to find tonal fabrics in as many textures as you can. Think shiny vs. matte, smooth vs. rough, etc. You can use scraps for this project, but if you are purchasing yardage, ¹/₄-yd/23-cm cuts should be fine.

❊❊❊❊❊❊❊ *TOOLS* ❊❊❊❊❊❊❊❊

- ➜ Fabric scissors
- ➜ Measuring tape
- ➜ Iron and ironing board
- ➜ Compass
- ➜ Tailor's chalk or air-soluble fabric marker
- ➜ Pencil
- ➜ Scrap paper
- ➜ Needle threader
- ➜ Embroidery needle, size 7 or 9
- ➜ Large embroidery hoop
- ➜ Staple gun with staples
- ➜ Sobo Craft & Fabric Glue

❊❊❊❊❊❊❊ *MATERIALS* ❊❊❊❊❊❊❊❊

- ➜ ½ yd/46 cm green linen
- ➜ 1¼ yd/1 m Heat 'n Bond Ultra or other double-sided fusible web
- ➜ 1 skein embroidery floss each, in white, yellow, light orange, light pink, bright orange, bright pink, and green
- ➜ 3 assorted white buttons (sew through, not shank style)
- ➜ 16-x-24-in/40.5-x-61-cm corkboard in a wood frame
- ➜ 2¼ yd/2 m ⅞-in/2.5-cm grosgrain ribbon, in green

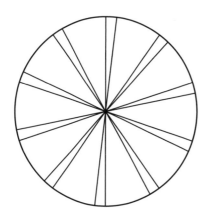

For the Lemon Slice

- ➜ One 9-in/23-cm square cotton twill, in yellow
- ➜ One 9-in/23-cm square cotton twill, in white
- ➜ One 9-x-12-in/23-x-30.5-cm piece wool felt, in yellow

For the Grapefruit Slice

- ➜ One 9-in/23-cm square silk Dupioni, in pink
- ➜ One 9-in/23-cm square cotton twill, in white, or the leftovers from the lemon's white cotton twill
- ➜ One 9-in/23-cm square cotton twill, in pink

For the Orange Slice:

- ➜ One 11-in/28-cm square linen, in orange
- ➜ One 9-in/23-cm square cotton twill, in white, or the leftovers from the lemon's white cotton twill
- ➜ One 9-in/23-cm square burlap, in orange

❊❊❊❊❊ *INSTRUCTIONS* ❊❊❊❊❊

1. Cut the piece of green linen to 18 x 26 in/46 x 66 cm.

2. Cut out nine 9-in/23-cm squares of double-sided fusible web. Fuse each piece to the back of 1 each of the lemon, grapefruit, and orange slice fabrics, following manufacturer's directions.

3. Lemon Slice: Use a compass to measure and then cut out an 8¼-in/21-cm circle from yellow twill, a 7½-in/19-cm circle from white twill, and a 7-in/18-cm circle from yellow felt. Fuse the white twill circle to the yellow twill circle. Using the chalk or marker, draw the lemon segments on the felt circle: the easiest way is to divide the circle into 8 to 10 segments and then take a little off each segment to make them irregular (please see sketch). Cut apart the segments. Arrange the lemon segments and fuse them to the white twill circle. If things are a little off center, that is just fine—it actually looks better if it's imperfect.

4. Grapefruit Slice: Cut an 8¼-in/21-cm circle from pink silk, a 7½-in/19-cm circle from white twill, and a 7-in/18-cm circle from pink twill. Fuse the white twill circle to the pink silk circle. Draw and cut apart the grapefruit segments from the pink twill circle (as detailed in step 3), then arrange the segments and fuse them to the white twill circle.

5. Orange Slice: The orange slice is a little different, as it will be only a partial circle. Draw a template circle on scrap paper that is 10½ in/26.5 cm in diameter. Cut off the top 2 in/5 cm of the circle and the left 2 in/5 cm. This is the basic template for the orange. Trace and cut this shape onto the orange linen. Then trace and cut the shape onto the white twill, and trim ½ in/12 mm off the curved edge. Trace and cut the shape onto the orange burlap, and trim ¾ in/2 cm off the curved edge. Fuse the white twill shape to the orange linen shape. Draw the orange segments on the orange burlap circle, and cut them apart (as detailed in step 3), then arrange and fuse them to the white twill shape.

6. Thread the embroidery needle with white floss. Use a running stitch or backstitch to embroider around the edge of the white twill portion of each fruit, slightly overlapping the "slices" (see photo).

7. Thread the embroidery needle with yellow floss and stitch down the center of each lemon segment. You can use a running stitch or just 1 big stitch for each segment. Repeat with light orange floss for the orange segments and light pink floss for the grapefruit segments.

8. Draw random circles on the green linen using the chalk or marker, varying the size and placement. Some may go off the edge—that's fine.

9. Place the green linen in the embroidery hoop and stitch over the circles drawn in step 8, using a running stitch or backstitch. Use a different color of floss for each circle.

10. Remove the embroidery hoop and lay the green linen flat. Arrange the citrus slices in a pleasing way on the linen, leaving a 1-in/2.5-cm border all the way around, and fuse them into place.

11. Thread your embroidery needle with bright orange floss. Use a running stitch or backstitch to embroider around the edge of the orange slice to secure it to the green linen. Repeat with bright pink floss for the grapefruit and yellow floss for the lemon. Sew a button onto the center of each slice using green floss.

12. Wrap the linen tightly around the corkboard and staple it to the back of the board into the wood frame. Glue the green ribbon around the edge of the frame to finish it off nicely and to hide any staples.

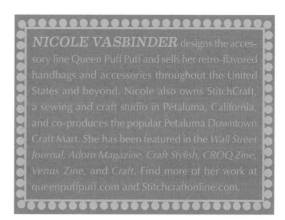

NICOLE VASBINDER designs the accessory line Queen Puff Puff and sells her retro-flavored handbags and accessories throughout the United States and beyond. Nicole also owns StitchCraft, a sewing and craft studio in Petaluma, California, and co-produces the popular Petaluma Downtown Craft Mart. She has been featured in the *Wall Street Journal*, *Adorn Magazine*, *Craft Stylish*, *CROQ Zine*, *Venus Zine*, and *Craft*. Find more of her work at queenpuffpuff.com and Stitchcraftonline.com.

Embroidered Snail Pillow

by Cathy Pitters

I have kind of a soft spot for snails in crafts—they're so cute. My mom appliquéd a big colorful snail on one of my tote bags when I was a little girl, and I loved it. With that bag in mind, I invited Cathy Pitters to stitch a snail. We really liked the look of the chunky chain stitches on a vintage pillow that I found at a flea market, and Cathy was excited to incorporate that style into her stitching.

TOOLS

+ Fabric scissors or rotary cutter
+ Compass
+ Measuring tape
+ Embroidered Snail Pillow templates (see templates)
+ Pencil
+ Tracing paper
+ Paper scissors
+ Straight pins
+ Blue painter's masking tape
+ Carbon transfer paper
+ Ballpoint pen
+ One 12-in/30.5-cm embroidery hoop
+ Embroidery needle, size 5
+ Sewing machine
+ Iron
+ Hand-sewing needle

MATERIALS

+ ²/₃ yd/61 cm cotton fabric, in solid color, for the pillow
+ Three 9-x-12-in/23-x-30.5-cm pieces wool felt, in complementary colors, for the snail body and shell
+ 5 skeins 3-ply wool embroidery yarn, in 5 coordinating colors
+ 1¹/₃ yd/121.5 cm rickrack trim
+ Thread to match cotton fabric
+ 12 oz/340 g bamboo fiberfill

P.S.

This project utilizes 3 stitch techniques: the chain stitch (linked and isolated), the backstitch, and the French knot. If you're not familiar with these stitches, a good resource is Jenny Hart's book *Embroidered Effects*. The chain stitch can be labor intensive and slow moving, but the end results are well worth the time and effort!

Don't care for the suggested color palette? Feel free to mix things up and use a color combination that suits your own tastes.

The yarn used for this project is 3-ply (3 strands twisted together) but has been separated and used 1 strand at a time. You can use more strands if you prefer thicker, fluffier stitches.

INSTRUCTIONS

1. Using the compass and scissors or rotary cutter, cut two 14¼-in/36-cm circles from the cotton for the front and back of the pillow. Cut a 4-x-44-in/10-x-112-cm strip of cotton for the pillow gusset.

2. Again using a compass, cut one 8½-in/21.5-cm circle from 2 different colors of felt. Cut a 4¼-in/11-cm circle out of the middle of one of the circles of felt. These felt circles will be layered to form the snail shell. Using a copier or scanner, enlarge the snail template by 167%. Print and, using tracing paper, trace the snail's body (kind of looks like a hot dog), with its eyes, smile, and antennae, from the template and cut it out. Pin this template to the third color of felt and cut it out. Hold on to this template for step 4.

3. Tape the intact felt circle to your work surface using painter's tape. Place the felt circle with a hole cut in the center on top of the first circle, and tape it down around the edges. Next center the embroidery design template over the felt circles and tape the top half securely in place, leaving the bottom half open.

Cut a piece of the carbon transfer paper into an 8½-in/21.5-cm square. Now slide this piece of transfer paper in between the embroidery template and felt circles, making sure there are no wrinkles in the paper. If needed, add a few extra pieces of tape to hold the transfer paper in place.

Using a ballpoint pen, trace over the embroidery design to transfer the pattern to the felt. Bear down heavily to be sure the impression comes through clearly. Remove the tape, then pin the felt circles together to form the snail shell.

4. Pin the snail shell to 1 of the cotton circles from step 1. Next, pin the snail body into place beneath the shell (refer to photo). Use the tape and transfer method detailed in step 3 to transfer the snail eye, smile, and antennae onto the fabric. This will be the pillow front.

5. Secure the pillow front into the embroidery hoop. Use 1 color of the embroidery yarn (#1) to backstitch around the outer edge of the snail shell, stitching through both layers of felt as well as the cotton. Use another shade of yarn (#2) to backstitch around the edge of the snail body, stitching through both felt and cotton layers.

6. Now that the felt is securely attached to the base fabric, you can begin adding the embellishing stitches. You should still keep some pins in place to make sure that the snail shell pieces don't shift. Working with 1 yarn color at a time will help keep things simple.

7. Using yarn color #2, chain stitch a looped design along the inside edge of the upper felt shell circle. This will secure the 2 shell pieces into place and make the rest of your stitching easier.

8. Using yarn color #1, chain stitch the snail antennae. Use the same color to chain stitch a small circular swirl in the very center of the snail shell. This is the center of the lazy daisy flower.

9. Select yarn color #3, and use it to backstitch the snail's smile. Use the same color to make a French knot for the snail's eye, then chain stitch a small circular swirl at the top of each antenna.

10. You can now begin working the 8 droplet shapes on the snail shell. Each droplet consists of 4 rows of chain stitching. Start by chain stitching the outermost row of all 8 droplets in yarn color #3. Select yarn color #4, and chain stitch the second row in that color; choose yarn color #5, and chain stitch the third row in that color. Finish by chain stitching the final inner row of all droplets with yarn color #3.

11. Still using yarn color #3, chain stitch the looped design along the outer edge of the shell's inner circle.

12. Using yarn color #5, create 8 isolated chain stitches to form a lazy daisy configuration with 8 petals around the very center dot on the snail shell. Use the same color to add 8 French knots around the outer edge of the shell's inner circle. The pillow front is done! Remove the pillow front from the embroidery hoop.

13. Line up the edge of the rickrack with the outer edge of the pillow front. Stitch down the center of the rickrack all around the outer edge of the pillow front, pinning rickrack into place if necessary.

14. Next you are going to attach the gusset piece you cut in step 1. Starting at the bottom part of the pillow front, pin 1 long edge of the 4-x-44-in/10-x-112-cm piece all along the outer edge of the pillow. Once the entire strip is pinned into place, pin together the 2 short ends of the fabric strip and sew that part closed. Using the stitch line from the rickrack sewn on in step 13, sew all around the circumference of the pillow front, removing the pins as you go.

15. Press the pillow with an iron (set to a very low temperature) to remove embroidery hoop marks and to make the rickrack lay flat.

16. With right sides together, pin the remaining fabric circle from step 1 all around the raw edge of the pillow gusset and stitch all around the circumference of the pillow, leaving a 5-in/12.5-cm opening at the bottom.

17. Turn the pillow right-side out and stuff it with bamboo fiberfill. Use a needle and thread to hand-stitch the opening closed.

CATHY PITTERS is a mom, artist, and seamstress. She runs the company Bossa Nova Baby (bossanovababy.com) out of her flamingo-pink craft bunker, where she creates handmade clothing and other fun oddities that she sells online and at fairs across the country. She also co-organizes Crafty Wonderland, Portland's twice-yearly art and craft extravaganza. She lives in Portland, Oregon, with her family.

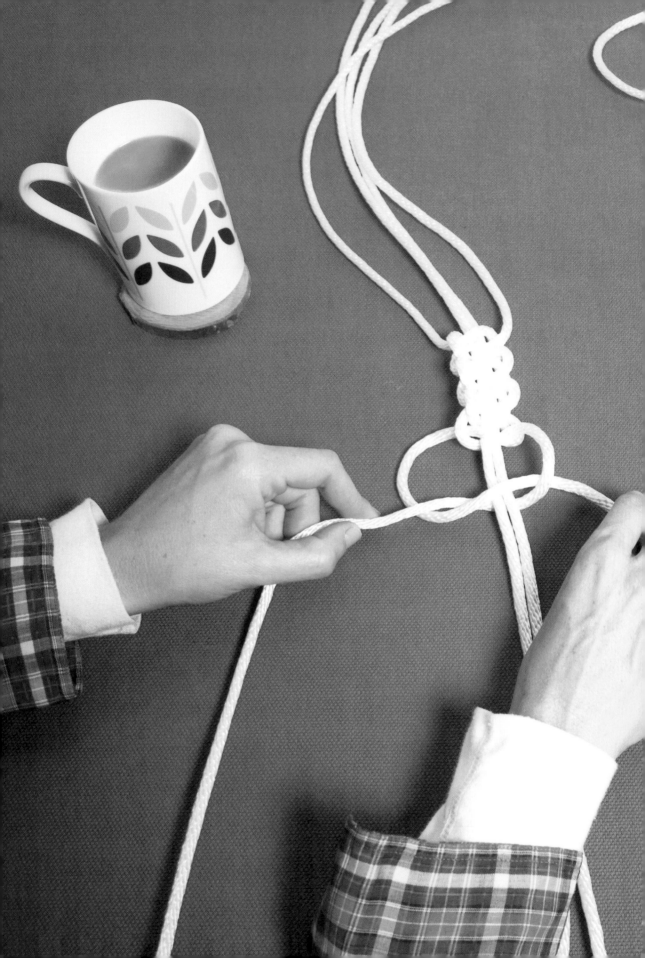

Chapter 4:
Craft Trends of the '60s and '70s:

Knots, Strings, Bottles, Rocks, and a Few Old Books

any crafts that were popular in the '60s and '70s had their roots in techniques that can be traced back hundreds of years. Terrariums, découpage, macramé, and stained glass are good examples. The reappearance of these crafts was marked by new approaches to both style and the use of materials. Many of these revivals were short-lived, though, and have unfortunately joined such other relics of the '70s as bellbottoms and 8-track tape players as shorthand for everything that was wrong with the period. This is unfortunate, and I think many of these craft techniques are due for some serious reevaluation.

In many ways the projects in this chapter do just that. The contributors have taken a look at some of the more clichéd craft projects of the era and have given them a very pleasing new twist. Macramé in particular has always been the punch line of many a bad joke about the '70s—it's easy to cringe at the sight of a big fuzzy overdone macramé plant hanger. But by simplifying the approach and using a cleaner looking material, macramé can look surprisingly contemporary and fresh. I say step outside your comfort zone and take a look at some of the more extreme crafts from the '60s and '70s. You might be surprised by the possibilities you discover!

Macramé and String Art from How to Make Plant Hangers *by Lynn Paulin, 1974 provided inspiration for Robert (see page 77) as well as Derek and Lauren (see facing page).*

Macramé Hanger

by Derek Fagerstrom and Lauren Smith

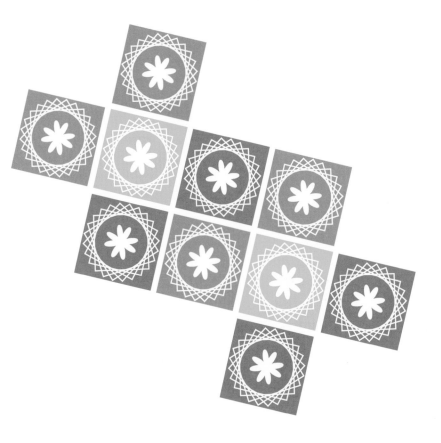

Macramé is one of the world's oldest crafts. It's the art of ornamental knotting and its development can be traced back to Turkish and Arabic cultures. In the '70s, people were seeking new ways to express themselves, and macramé gained popularity because it was an easy and inexpensive way to create exotic home ornaments and fashion accessories from simple materials. Big chunky plant hangers made with heavy jute cording and rustic wooden beads probably come to mind when you think of macramé.

Derek Fagerstrom and Lauren Smith have breathed new life into macramé by using nautical rope and clean simple knots to create this plant hanger. It's a great way to get started with macramé, and once you're hooked and are ready to learn more, you can find dozens of vintage instruction books on eBay.

TOOLS

- → Measuring tape
- → Scissors

MATERIALS
(PER HANGER)

- → 96 ft/29.5 m cotton rope (such as 2 packs of Venetian blind cord: 48 ft x ⁹/₆₄ in/14.5 m x 3.5 mm braided cotton)
- → One 1½-in/4-cm metal ring
- → 1 ceiling hook
- → 1 flowerpot (we used Eco Forms brand)

INSTRUCTIONS

1. Measure and cut 6 lengths of rope that are 16 ft/5 m long each.

2. Feed the 6 lengths of rope through the metal ring, folding the rope in the middle so you have 12 equal lengths of rope hanging down from the metal ring.

3. Take 1 piece of rope and wrap it horizontally around the rest of the rope a few times near the ring. Pull the end down through the final loop to secure the loops.

4. Ask a friend to hold onto the ring, or attach the ring to something sturdy like a door knob.

5. Separate the strands into 3 groups of 4 to create your 3 hanging chains, also known as *sennits*.

6. Each sennit has 4 ropes. Separate them so you have 2 sets of 2 ropes and follow the illustrations to tie 3 or 4 Josephine knots down the length of each sennit.

7. To create the final Josephine knots, take 2 strands from 1 sennit and 2 strands from an adjacent sennit, and knot them together. Repeat 2 more times with the remaining sennits.

8. Determine where you want your planter to sit and gather all the loose ends at that spot, wrapping 1 piece of rope around the bunch and securing them together as you did in step 3.

9. Tie a knot at the end of each piece of rope and trim off any excess rope.

10. Insert a hook into your ceiling and hang your planter by slipping the metal ring over the hook.

DEREK FAGERSTROM & LAUREN SMITH are the owners of the Curiosity Shoppe and gallery in San Francisco, where they offer crafts, kits, and curios for the creatively inclined. They are the authors of *Show Me How* and *Wallpaper Projects*, and are frequent contributors to a number of design blogs and publications. Visit them at Curiosityshoppeonline.com.

Birdcage String Art

by Robert Mahar

String art was originally devised as a way to teach geometry to children and is attributed to self-taught nineteenth-century mathematician Mary Everest Boole, one of very few women in the field of mathematics at the time. It became popular as a craft technique in the late '60s, and geometric imagery gave way to figurative forms in the '70s, such as owls, sailing ships, snails, and more.

The technique involves a series of nails that are carefully driven into a board in a precise formation, with string then twisted around each nail to create a geometric design. Abstract op art patterns are still probably the most commonly seen subject matter. I asked Robert Mahar if he would like to try his hand at string art and he came up with this new and fresh perspective. I just love the little fabric birds he added.

TOOLS

- Mod Podge
- One 2-in-/5-cm-wide foam brush
- Fabric scissors
- Birdcage String Art patterns and template (see templates)
- Blue painter's masking tape
- Needle-nose pliers
- Hammer
- Ruler
- Chopstick (optional)
- Paper scissors
- Disappearing ink fabric marker
- Small paintbrush
- Sobo Craft & Fabric glue
- Tweezers (optional)

MATERIALS

- One 8-x-8-x-½-in/20-x-20-cm-x-12-mm uncradled natural maple art board
- One 9½-in/24-cm square linen, in taupe, for the background (Tip: Spray the fabric with starch and iron it prior to measuring and cutting, to make it easier to handle.)
- Fifty-two ⅞-in/2.5-cm wire brads (18-gauge)
- One 4-in/10-cm square linen, in robin's egg blue, for the birds
- One 3-in/7.5-cm square linen, in cream, for the birds
- 1 spool Coats & Clark Button & Carpet Thread, in black

INSTRUCTIONS

1. Lightly and evenly coat the face and sides of the board with Mod Podge using a foam brush. Press the coated board firmly facedown onto the center of the taupe linen, making sure it is even and aligned. Smooth the fabric with your fingers to eliminate bubbles or wrinkles. Wrap the fabric around the sides of the board and apply more Mod Podge to secure it around the back. Snip off excess fabric at the side and back of each corner. Allow to dry.

2. Photocopy the birds and wings from the birdcage string art template. These will act as your templates for the fabric birds you will create in step 4. Then, position the birdcage string art pattern with the numbered dots on the fabric and secure it with painter's tape. Position the first nail over a dot near the center of the pattern, hold it vertical with pliers, and use a hammer to lightly tap the nail through the paper and into the board until it is approximately ½ in/12 mm tall. Repeat this step for every dot on the pattern, working from the center of the pattern out. Check your brads often from various angles, making certain they are vertically as straight as possible.

TIP: Mark a ½-in/12-mm line on the side of a chopstick to use as a guide so it will be easier to maintain the ½-in/12-mm uniform height of the brads.

3. Peel off the tape and carefully loosen the pattern from the edges, working it up the brads and lifting it off the top. Keep this pattern; you'll need to reference it starting with step 5.

4. Cut out your bird and wing template pieces, and use them to trace the shapes onto the blue and cream linens. Refer to the image of the finished project for placement and position the pieces in place. Use the small paintbrush to apply a thin layer of glue to the back of each bird piece and secure it in place. Allow it to dry.

TIP: Tweezers make it easier to handle and position the tiny, glue-coated fabric pieces of the bird design.

5. Tie 1 yard of thread to brad A, leaving a 4-in/10-cm tail secured to the board with painter's tape. Holding the thread taut at all times, wrap it clockwise completely around brad B; repeat clockwise wrapping around brads C, D, E and F; then loop around brad G; re-wrap clockwise completely around brad F; across to E, D, C, B; and re-tie to brad A.

This first chain of strung thread creates the back outline of the birdcage's base. Do not trim off the remaining long tail (the end that is not taped down); rather set it aside to be used to create the front outline of the birdcage's base in step 8. Gently press this chain of strung thread close to the base of the brads.

TIP: Dab a tiny amount of the fabric glue on the tied thread knots to secure and prevent unraveling.

6. Leaving the thread attached to the spool, tie the loose end around brad P, again leaving a 4-in/10-cm tail secured to the board with painter's tape. Loop the thread around brads in the following pattern: P to G, G to O, O to F, F to N, N to E, E to M, M to D, D to L, L to C, C to K, K to B, B to J, J to A, A to I, I to P, P to H, H to O, O to G, G to N, N to F, F to M, M to E, E to L, L to D, D to K, K to C, C to J, J to B, B to I, I to A, A to H, H to P.

7. Tie off at brad P and cut the excess thread. The resulting starburst pattern of strung thread creates the base or bottom of the birdcage. To create the illusion of depth and forced perspective, gently press the thread looped around brads A through G down towards the base of the brads.

8. Return to the long tail (remaining from step 5) of thread tied off at brad A. From brad A, wrap this tail clockwise completely around brad P; continue wrapping around brads O, N, M, L, K, J, I, H; then loop around brad G; re-wrap clockwise completely around brad H; back across to I, J, K, L, M, N, O, P; re-tie to brad A and cut thread.

9. The birdcage bars, open door, and top hanging-loop are all created from 1 continuous piece of thread. Leaving the thread attached to the spool, tie the loose end around brad 1, again leaving a 4-in/10-cm tail secured to the board with masking tape. Holding the thread taut at all times, wrap it clockwise completely around brads 2, 3, 4, 5, 6 and loop around brad P; re-wrap clockwise completely back up around brads 6, 5, 4, 3, 2 and 1. This chain of strung thread creates the first bar of the birdcage.

10. The second bar of the birdcage extends from brads 1 to 7, 8, 9, 10, 11, B to N and back up to brad 1. The third bar of the birdcage extends from brads 1 to 12, 13, 14, 15, C to M and back up to brad 1. The fourth and center bar of the birdcage extends from brads 1 to 16, 17, D to L and back up to brad 1. The fifth bar of the birdcage extends from brads 1 to 18, 19, 20, 21, E to K and back up to brad 1. The sixth bar of the birdcage extends from brads 1 to 22, 23, 24, 25, 26, F to J and back up to brad 1.

11. The seventh and final bar of the birdcage extends from brads 1 to 27, 28, 29, 30, 31 to loop around H, back up to 31, and then extends left to create the birdcage's crossbar. Wrap thread clockwise completely from brads 31 to 26, 21, 17, 15, 11 to loop around brad 6, re-wrap back across to brads 11, 15, 17, 21, 26, 31. Then to create the birdcage door, wrap to brad 32, 33, and loop around brad 30; re-wrap back around 33, 32, 31; then up to brad 30 and extend left again to create the birdcage's second crossbar to brads 25, 20, 16, 14, and 10; to loop around brad 5 back across to brads 10, 14, 16, 20, 25, and 30. Continue back up to the top of the birdcage around brads 29, 28, 27, and 1. To create the illusion of an open birdcage door, press the string on 32 and 33 close to the base of the brads.

12. Finally create the birdcage's hanging-loop by continuing to wrap from 1 to 34, 35, 36 to loop around 1 and back to 36, 35, 34 and tie off at brad 1 and cut thread.

ROBERT MAHAR was one of those kids who preferred staying indoors to weave potholders on a plastic loom and bake Shrinky-Dinks to running around the yard. As an adult, he continues his crafty pursuits as the proprietor and ringleader of Mahar Drygoods (Mahardrygoods.com), the online emporium of vintage and artisan-crafted curiosities for children. He has been a guest on *The Martha Stewart Show*.

Painted Stone Paperweights

by Jill Bliss

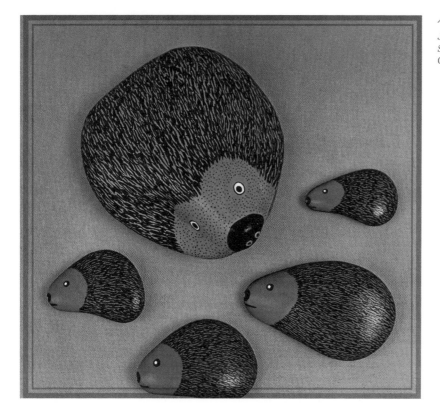

Found in *The Beautiful Crafts Book* are some surprisingly beautiful photos of stones painted as fish, hedgehogs, and turtles. These reminded me of the ladybugs that my Brownie troop used to make. We would go into the schoolyard garden and select just the right stone that inspired us. The troop leader helped us spray-paint them red and then we decorated them ourselves.

Since nature figures prominently in Jill Bliss's work, I thought she would have an interesting take on this project. Jill said it best herself: "Vintage crafts are a good starting point for modern-day projects!" Jill used paint pens and chose not to cover the entire stone with paint so that the natural beauty of the stone became part of the design.

TOOLS

→ Pencil (optional)
→ Painted Stone Paperweights templates (see templates)

MATERIALS

→ Four 1½- to 3-in/4- to 7.5-cm stones, with a fairly flat and smooth surface on 1 side
→ Paint Pens (as shown in black, white, red, orange, and lime green)
→ Varnish (optional)

INSTRUCTIONS

1. Rinse off the stones as needed and allow them to dry completely.

TIP: Use the shape of your stone as a guide in choosing the imagery. Jill chose animal life: starfish, anemones, a snail, and a ladybug.

2. If you like, use the templates provided as a guide to sketch your design on a stone first using a pencil. Or just go for it with the paint pens. You might want to try out a few "practice" stones first.

3. Allow paint to dry according to package directions.

4. If you feel you want a glossy coat, you can spray or paint your rocks with the varnish of your choice.

TIP: Use the point of your paint pen to create a dotted effect—as you see on the ladybug, snail, and starfish.

Originally from Northern California, **JILL BLISS** is an artist, designer, and crafter who now calls Portland, Oregon, home. She uses sustainable products as much as possible, and hopes to inspire others to create a more thoughtful art and design industry that focuses on local economies, fair practices, reusable materials, and less consumption. Her work can be found at Jillbliss.com.

Recycled Bottle Wind Chime

by Billie Lopez and Tootie Maldonado

///

Billie and Tootie's inspiration: Wind Chimes from Bottle Cutting and Decoration, *1972.*

I gave my dad a Ronco Bottle and Jar cutter for Christmas one year, as seen on TV. I guess I thought it would be cool for him to make glasses out of old soda and beer bottles.

Unfortunately, my dad tried to use it once and gave up in frustration because it was not made very well, so it sat on his tool bench gathering dust for years. Luckily Billie and Tootie had much more success with their bottle cutter and have created this amazing wind chime. The hand-painted bit of color adds a nice touch.

- ➜ Ephrem's Bottle Cutter Kit
- ➜ Sandpaper in a fine, fine grade (#150) for sanding and smoothing and (#1000 to 1200) for polishing
- ➜ Shallow paper bowls, 1 per paint color
- ➜ Large hand-sewing needle
- ➜ Craft glue

MATERIALS

- ➜ 6 to 8 clear glass bottles, in various shapes and sizes
- ➜ Two to three 2-oz/60-ml bottles high-gloss acrylic paint or special-purpose glass paint for outdoor use, in complementary colors (such as Liquitex "Glossies")
- ➜ About 18 yards garden twine
- ➜ 6 to 8 wine bottle–size cork stoppers (available at craft stores)

P.S.

Larger corks can also be shaved down to fit smaller bottles if needed.

INSTRUCTIONS

1. Select your bottles. We went with clear in assorted sizes but made sure that they all had nice contoured shapes. You probably have just the right ones in your recycling bin.

2. Cut and sand your bottles according to the bottle-cutter kit instructions. Cut the bottles at varied lengths, taking the size and shape of the bottle into consideration.

3. Now you're ready to add some color. Squirt your paint into the paper bowls, filling each bowl approximately ½ in/12 mm. Dilute the bowls of paint with water by approximately 25%. Blend well. Diluting this much will give you a watercolor effect. If you prefer a more solid look, use less water. Dip the bottom of each bottle into a bowl of paint. We went about ¼ in/6 mm deep with our paint but you can cover as much of your bottle as desired. Set the paint according to package instructions.

4. Thread the large needle with the twine. Carefully string the twine through the vertical center of each cork. Use generous amounts of twine on each cork (several feet) so that you have plenty of room to hang your bottles at your desired length. Leave a 2- to 3-in/5- to 7.5-cm length of twine at the end of your corks (this will be inside of your bottle), and tie a knot in each end of the twine, for each cork.

TIP: If you prefer to stack some of your bottles, you will have to attach 1 bottle to the first cork before stringing the next cork to the same length of twine.

5. Once your bottles are set and dry, you can attach them to the corks. For extra security you can add a bit of glue to the cork where it meets the mouth of the bottle.

6. Make sure your bottles hang closely enough to one another so that they will gently clang together in the wind. Please refer to the photograph of the finished project for inspiration on how to space your bottles.

BILLIE LOPEZ AND **TOOTIE MALDONADO** were both born and raised in Los Angeles. Friends since high school, they talked about the idea of opening their own shop together for years. In 2005 they started ReForm School in a small corner of a friend's boutique in Echo Park. The shop is a reflection of three of their favorite things: art, craft, and design, with an emphasis on handmade and sustainable materials. ReForm School in now located in the Sunset Junction area of Silver Lake and can be found at Reformschoolrules.com.

Folded-Book Hanging Sculptures

by Lucy Spriggs

///

Lucy's inspiration: Cover of
Projects Made of Folded
Magazines, *1966.*

I remember making a turkey out of an old *TV Guide* as a Girl Scout. Each page was folded, fanned out, and then painted brown. I added a foam ball for the head and probably some pom-poms and feathers for decoration. Memories of this project flooded back to me when I found a copy of *Projects Made of Folded Magazines—A Craft "How-To" Create Book by Aleene*.

When I showed it to Lucy Spriggs, she really loved all of the characters, ladies, and animals made from folded magazines. She was inspired to make something using the technique, but wanted to do something more minimal—that perhaps looked a little more grown-up and modern. We thought it would be interesting to use old books for this project; if they are a little yellowed, then all the better. We liked the beautiful color of the aged paper and decided that painting them was unnecessary.

TOOLS

→ Folding diagrams (see facing page)
→ X-Acto knife
→ Hot glue gun and glue stick
→ Compass
→ Paper scissors
→ Ruler
→ Large needle
→ Aleene's Tacky Glue

MATERIALS

→ 3 secondhand books, preferably 500 pages plus (Tip: Paperback books are a little easier to handle.)
→ One 3-x-4-in/7.5-x-10-cm piece lightweight cardboard (more or less depending on book spine; see step 5)
→ String or twine

INSTRUCTIONS

1. Use the X-Acto knife to cut off the front and back covers of each book at the edge of spine.

2. Following the diagram(s) for each book, fold all pages as indicated. The diagrams are to create the hanging sculptures shown in the photo of the completed project, page 86. Feel free to create your own variations for other shapes.

Book 1, (see page 86, left): Refer to figures 1 and 2. Alternate these folds as desired to create the "star" shape. Lucy alternated her folds every 4 pages.

Book 2, (see page 86, center): Refer to figure 3. Do this fold on every page of your book.

Book 3, (see page 86, right): Refer to figures 4 to 7. Fold each page following figures 4 to 7 and repeat for all pages of your book to create the "lantern" shape.

TIP: Fold each page as close to the center of the book as possible. This keeps the shape the same all the way around.

3. Stand the book up and let the pages fan out (to make it look "in the round").

4. Apply hot glue to each long edge of the spine and press them together. The spine itself will now be rounded, thus creating a hole that runs down the center.

5. Using a compass and scissors, cut six ¾- to 1-in/2- to 2.5-cm circles of lightweight cardboard (the exact measurements will be dictated by the size of the top and bottom openings of the books) and punch small holes in the centers using the large needle.

6. Cut your desired length of string or twine (depending on the ceiling height), string a few inches through 1 of the cardboard circles, and make a knot (this will be a "stopper" at the bottom). Take the long end of the twine, string it through the center of the book and through the other cardboard circle, and knot it again (thus creating the top "stopper").

7. Add a few drops of Aleene's Tacky Glue under each "stopper" to secure.

Book 1

fig. 1   fig. 2

LUCY SPRIGGS runs Ivanhoe Books, a small art and design bookstore in the Silver Lake neighborhood of Los Angeles. Her mother was a high school art teacher for years, so she grew up around arts, crafts, and glue guns. Lucy is an avid quilter, sockmonkey maker, and window-display designer. Find her musings at Ivanhoebooks.blogspot.com.

Book 2

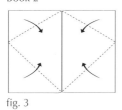

fig. 3

Book 3

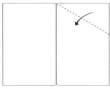

fig. 4

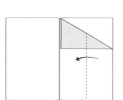

fig. 5

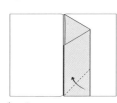

fig. 6

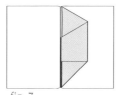

fig. 7

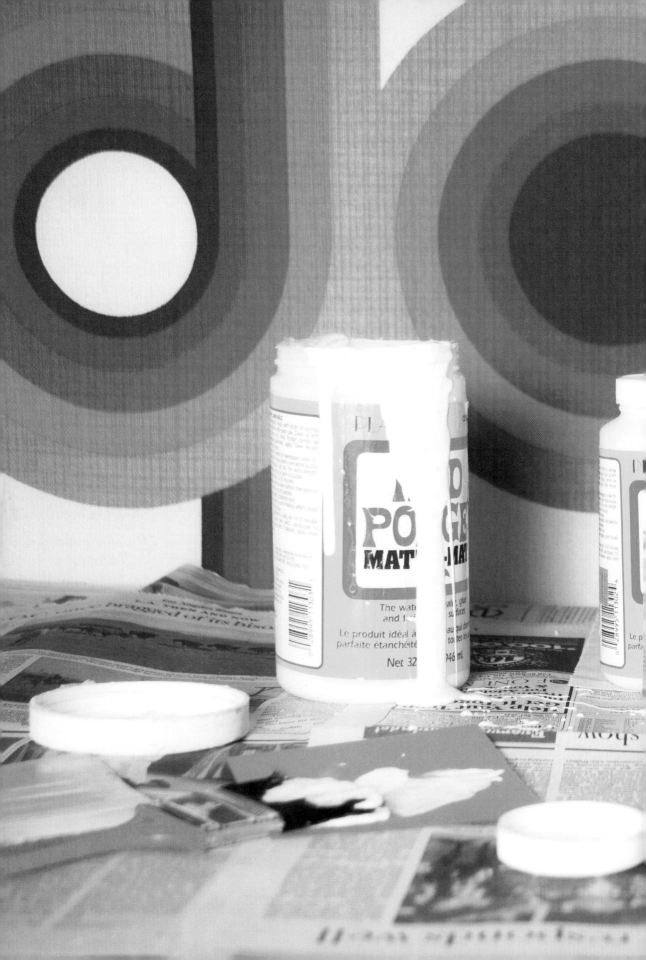

Chapter 5:
Create with Paper

Cover of Rags to Riches with
Mod Podge *by Jan Meyerson
Wetstone circa early '70s.*

There isn't a more versatile material for crafts than paper. Inexpensive and unpretentious, paper invites the crafter to explore the range of its possibilities today just as it did in the '60s and '70s. This chapter explores some of the many uses of paper in crafts, from découpage to handmade gift wrap and stationery. For a classic découpage project, check out Katie Hanburger's magazine holder on page 105. Crafting with paper never goes out of style!

Patricia Nimocks: Craft Revivalist

One day while shopping at a thrift store, I discovered a cache of "Patricia Nimocks Decorative Hardware." The packages contained the hangers, knobs, and corner protectors that were meant to be used for découpage projects. I remember my mom having something of an obsession with découpage when I was growing up, and one of the walls of our living room had at least a dozen of her creations on display. Many of them had little antique-looking doodads attached to them, which very well may have been Patricia Nimocks products.

Découpage involves the decoration of an object with paper cut-outs, which are then varnished or lacquered. Though it had its roots in the eighteenth century, it enjoyed a huge popular revival in the '60s due in no small part to the efforts of Patricia Nimocks. She is credited with repopularizing découpage, introducing the technique to a broad new audience of home crafters and do-it-yourselfers. Patricia decided to start her own craft company at the age of forty after a career in art restoration. She took the skills and techniques she had used as a professional and found ways of making them accessible to the public. She had some of the materials she used in art restoration reformulated for the consumer market, and her popular spray varnish is still sold today.

Jan Meyerson Wetstone: Inventor of Mod Podge

Découpage was very appealing to interior decorators in the '60s, none more so than Jan Meyerson Wetstone, who owned an interior design shop in Atlanta, Georgia. Though she liked the aesthetic effect of découpage, Jan found it to be a little too time consuming—a busy decorator really had no time to brush on all of those layers of varnish. So she went out to her garage, did a bit of experimenting, and came up with the now-famous mixture for Mod Podge, which is short for "Modern Découpage." With Mod Podge one could achieve the visual effect of découpage relatively easily and quickly. Jan tested her new product on all kinds of surfaces, even découpaging bed sheets to a VW Bug. Due to demand from her customers, she started selling Mod Podge kits, and the rest is history.

Festive Gift Boxes

by Susie and Heidi Bauer

When I saw this closet full of fun gift-wrap ideas in a mid-'60s issue of *Better Homes and Gardens*, I knew that Susie and Heidi, who also pull tons of inspiration from this era, would be excited. They took the idea and ran with it, creating their own array of updated wrappings. Beautiful gift wrap can leave a lasting impression, so have fun and get creative with this project.

- Paper scissors
- Pencil
- X-Acto knife
- Aleene's Tacky Glue
- Scotch tape
- Glue stick
- Hot glue gun and glue sticks
- Self-adhesive foam mounting squares (in the scrap-book section at craft stores)

Lock and Key Variation:

TOOLS

- Festive Gift Boxes templates (see templates)

MATERIALS

- One 8½-x-11-in/21.5-x-28-cm sheet card stock, in light pink, for lock and key
- 1 small piece card stock, in yellow, for heart
- 1 small piece card stock, in dark pink, for keyhole
- One 10-x-12-x-3-in/25-x-30.5-x-7.5-cm (sweater-size) gift box
- Solid wrapping paper, in orange
- One 9-x-11-in/23-x-28-cm piece patterned wrapping or craft paper, in pink (Tip: Use a recycled or scrap piece of patterned paper from another craft project.)
- 27 in/68.5 cm 1-in/2.5-cm ribbon, in light pink
- 10 in/25 cm ½-in/12-mm ribbon, in dark pink

INSTRUCTIONS

1. Cut out the lock, key, and heart templates (including the keyhole on the lock and the center of the key), and trace them onto the card stock with a pencil: light pink for the key and lock, yellow for the heart. Cut the pieces from the card stock with scissors or the X-Acto knife. Using glue, adhere a square of dark pink card stock on the back of the cut-out lock so it shows through the keyhole.

2. Wrap the gift box in the solid wrapping paper using Scotch tape.

3. Cut a piece from the patterned wrapping or craft paper to make a panel just for the front of the box. Use a glue stick to mount the patterned panel to the front of the gift box.

4. Thread the paper "lock" onto the 27 in/68.5 cm length of 1-in/2.5-cm ribbon and lay the lock on the patterned-paper panel, wrapping the ribbon around the middle of the box, to the back. Secure the ribbon on the back of the box with hot glue.

5. Remove the backing from 1 side of several self-adhesive foam mounting squares, and affix them to the back of the paper key, around the loop and down the shaft, spacing the squares about 1 in/2.5 cm apart.

TIP: The paper key could be glued down to the box with a glue stick, but the foam squares will "pop" the key away from the surface of the box and add dimension.

6. Remove backing from the other side of the foam mounting squares and place the key next to the lock, overlapping the ribbon. Gently press down to adhere the adhesive.

7. On the back of the heart, affix 3 foam mounting squares, and then place the heart in the center of the key loop and adhere.

8. Using the ½-in/12-mm ribbon, make a pretty bow that is approximately 3 in/7.5 cm wide. Trim the ends.

9. Using hot glue, attach the ribbon to the top of the key.

Flower Vase Variation:

TOOLS

→ Festive Gift Boxes template (see templates)

MATERIALS

→ One 8½-x-11-in/21.5-x-28-cm sheet card stock, in light yellow
→ One 14½-x-7½-x-5-in/37-x-19-x-12.5-cm (shoebox-size) gift box
→ Striped wrapping paper, in pastel colors (Tip: Use recycled wrapping paper and scraps of ribbon left over from other craft projects.)
→ Three 7-in/18-cm lengths ⅜-in/1-cm grosgrain ribbon, in green
→ 18 in/46 cm ⅜-in/1-cm satin ribbon, in pink
→ Three 1-in/2.5-cm paper candy cups, in orange
→ Three 1-in/2.5-cm paper candy cups, in yellow

INSTRUCTIONS

1. Cut out the Flower Vase template, and use the pencil to trace it onto light yellow card stock. Cut out using scissors or the X-Acto knife.

2. Wrap the gift box with the wrapping paper using Scotch tape.

3. Referring to the photo of the completed project as a guide for placement, arrange the 3 pieces of green ribbon as "stems" on the front of the box and secure them using hot glue.

4. Tie the pink ribbon in a bow around the narrow part of the vase. Position the bow on the front of the vase. Trim the ribbon to make a tidy bow.

5. Remove the backing from 1 side of several mounting squares, and affix them around the back of the vase, spacing them about 1 in/2.5 cm apart. Remove the backing from the other side of the mounting squares, and place the vase on the front of the box, overlapping the ribbon stems. Gently press down to adhere.

TIP: The paper vase could be glued down to the box with a glue stick, but the foam squares will "pop" the vase away from the surface of the box and add dimension.

6. For the flowers, nest 2 contrasting colors of paper candy cups and, using a small amount of hot glue, adhere the cups together into 1 "flower." Once the glue is dry, gently spread out the 2 cups to make flower petals.

7. Glue 1 flower to the top of each of the ribbon stems.

Sisters, best friends, and business partners *SUSIE* and *HEIDI BAUER* were born in Los Angeles's San Fernando Valley in the late '60s. The children of European immigrants, they grew up obsessed with pop culture and the mass-produced objects of the era. This became the inspiration for the designs they produce for their stationery company Rock Scissor Paper (Rockscissorpaper.com).

Tissue Paper Painting Tray

by Tom Early

When it comes to the use of tissue paper and its cousin crepe paper in crafts, paper flowers are usually the first thing to come to mind, but there's much more you can do with them. The inspiration for this decorated platter comes from an article called "New Tissue Paper Painting" that appeared in a 1961 edition of *McCall's Needlework and Crafts*. The basic idea was to paint household items white, apply colorful tissue paper, and add gold painted details by hand.

    I showed the article to Tom Early and he was excited to take on the project because he saw it as a way to combine his love of painting, color, and graphic '60s imagery. Tom took the technique a step further by covering the entire surface in tissue paper to give it an interesting overall texture. You would never know that there's a pizza pan under there.

TOOLS

- ➜ Paper scissors
- ➜ One 1-in-/2.5-cm-wide flat paintbrush
- ➜ Pencil
- ➜ Drafting compass (with pencil tip)
- ➜ Tissue Paper Painting Tray templates (see templates)
- ➜ Small paintbrush (for details)
- ➜ Straightedge ruler (optional)

MATERIALS

- ➜ One 15-in/38-cm round aluminum pizza pan
- ➜ 1 can matte spray paint, in white, for covering pizza pan
- ➜ Tissue paper (non bleed), in white, and as shown or as desired
- ➜ One 4-oz/120-ml bottle Liquitex brand matte medium
- ➜ 1 tube gouache paint, in gold, for accents
- ➜ 1 tube gouache paint, in white, for accents
- ➜ Spray-on crystal clear lacquer paint

INSTRUCTIONS

1. Paint the front and back of the pizza pan with the white spray paint. Allow the paint to dry according to the manufacturer's instructions. One coat should be fine, but do 2 if needed.

2. Either cut or tear strips of white tissue paper. Using the 1-in/2.5-cm paintbrush, apply a thin layer of the matte medium to the pan and lay down the strips of tissue paper for desired texture and thickness. Allow to dry.

TIP: To tear the tissue paper, you can do so free-hand or lay your tissue paper on your work surface and lay a straightedge ruler on top to use as a guide as you tear the paper. You will get a cleaner line this way.

3. Locate the center of the tray and mark it with a pencil. Using the compass, draw concentric circles at 3, 6½ , 9½, and 11 in/7.5, 16.5, 24, and 28 cm.

4. Using the triangle templates, cut the shapes out of the colored tissue paper. You may follow the colors and shapes as seen in the photo or you may use colors of your choice.

5. Apply another layer of matte medium to the pan, and apply the tissue paper shapes, using the pencil circles as your guide. Let dry.

6. Using gouache and the small paintbrush, add accents in gold and white, using the photo of the project as your guide. Let the paint dry.

7. Spray the pan with crystal clear lacquer paint for protective coating.

TOM EARLY is a native of Newport Beach, California, and he studied painting at Art Center College of Design. Like many who grew up in Southern California, Tom is influenced by the talented designers who worked for Walt Disney, especially Mary Blair and Rolly Crump. He is an Emmy Award–winning set decorator for the daytime drama *The Days of Our Lives*, and splits his time between Pasadena and Palm Springs.

Scrap Notes Stationery

by Meg Mateo Ilasco

People who create also have a tendency to save things, and having a stash of materials at hand always helps when you need to come up with something at a moment's notice. These "scrap notes" are just that: they're made using scraps left over from other projects and they can be made in a matter of minutes. I love how Meg took inspiration for this project from the '70s and gave it a more contemporary feel, but still kept the spirit of the time period in her use of color.

TOOLS

- → X-Acto knife
- → Cutting mat
- → Straightedge ruler
- → Scrap Notes Stationery templates (see templates)
- → Tracing paper
- → Pencil
- → Fine-tip scissors
- → Clear craft glue (in a bottle with a sharp nozzle)
- → Paper towels
- → Tweezers (optional, to aid in placement of embroidery floss)

MATERIALS

- → 3 or 4 sheets card stock, in various colors
- → Embroidery floss, in various colors
- → 20 in/50 cm medium acrylic yarn, in yellow, for the sun

INSTRUCTIONS

1. Using the X-Acto knife, cutting mat, and straightedge, trim the card stock to the size you want. Standard sizes shown here are 4½ x 6¼ in/11.5 x 16 cm (fits an A6 envelope) and 5½ x 8½ in/14 x 21 cm (fits an A9 envelope).

2. To make the car, horse, or peapod designs, select a design from those provided on the templates, and place the tracing paper on top of the illustration. Using a pencil, trace the outlined shape. Do not trace the filled-in shapes.

3. Flip the tracing paper over and position the design on a card. On the reverse side of the tracing paper, trace over the outline with pencil. This will lightly transfer the design to your card.

4. Choose embroidery floss in a color that contrasts with your card. Using the fine-tip scissors, trim your embroidery floss to 18 in/46 cm. Set aside.

5. You will apply glue and attach embroidery floss in small sections. With the sharp nozzle of your clear craft-glue bottle, place a small amount of glue along a 1-in/2.5-cm section of your outlined design. Wipe the tip of the nozzle with a paper towel to remove any excess glue.

6. Place the embroidery floss on top of the glue. Using tweezers may help here. Press down gently with only your fingernail.

7. Repeat steps 5 and 6 until you have applied embroidery floss to the entire design. Trim any excess floss with the scissors.

8. To make the hands/sun card, and for the parts of the car, horse, and peapod designs that use cut-out pieces of paper, place tracing paper on top of the illustration. Using a pencil, trace the solid shapes.

9. Choose colored card stock that will contrast with your card for the cut-out pieces. Flip the card stock over so any texture is facing down. Flip the tracing paper over and place it on the backside of the card stock. Trace over your pencil markings using pencil to transfer the design to the card stock. Using your scissors, cut along the traced outline.

10. Place a small amount of glue on the backside of each of your cut-out forms and place them on your card, following the placement on the templates.

11. To make the tail on the horse, cut four 3-in/7.5-cm pieces of embroidery floss and knot them in the middle. Trim the ends of the embroidery floss to about 1 in/2.5 cm. Place a small amount of glue on the knot and attach it to the horse.

12. To make the sun (above the hands), take 1 end of the yarn and coil it around itself. Place glue on the backside of the coiled form and place it on your card.

MEG MATEO ILASCO is a designer, illustrator, and writer in the San Francisco Bay Area. She began creating handmade stationery eleven years ago as a wedding invitation designer. She is now the principal of Mateo Ilasco (mateoilasco.com), a stationery and home accessories company, as well as the author of several books, including *Craft, Inc.*, *Creative, Inc.*, and *Crafting a Meaningful Home*.

Découpaged Magazine Holder

by Katie Hanburger

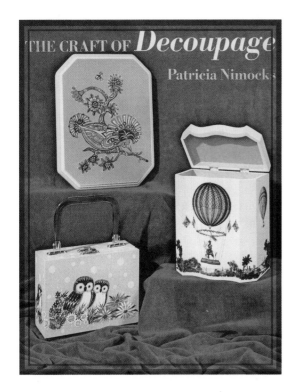

As a graphic designer who silkscreens her own designs, Katie Hanburger tends to accumulate lots of little pieces of leftover paper and scraps from her various projects, and she saves them just in case she can use them later. For this project, she assembled some of her favorite design remnants—test prints on newsprint, old drawings, and linoleum prints. Using these leftover pieces makes Katie's project very personal, and you can follow her example. Think about what you might have in your paper stash that you could use in similar ways.

TOOLS

→ Fine-grit sandpaper (#180–#100)
→ Acrylic paintbrush (optional)
→ Foam brushes in assorted sizes
→ Scissors (optional)
→ Mod Podge (matte)
→ Brayer (optional)
→ Paper towels

MATERIALS

→ 1 unfinished birch plywood magazine holder (as shown: the KNUFF file from IKEA)
→ Acrylic paint (optional)
→ Decorative papers, in various sizes and shapes (Tip: leftovers from screen-printing projects, assorted patterned papers, drawings, linoleum prints, etc. work well. You may also use one of Katie's original designs [in the template section] to incorporate into your project by either scanning it [play around with size and color] so that you can use it multiple times or cutting it out as-is for single use.)
→ Krylon Workable Fixatif spray
→ Krylon UV-Resistant Clear Acrylic Coating spray (matte)

P.S.

Almost any unfinished wood object is a suitable starting point for découpage. Just remember to consider how the object will be used.

INSTRUCTIONS

1. Lightly sand the magazine holder with the sandpaper to eliminate any small snags or rough spots that might exist. Brush off the wood dust.

2. If you choose to paint the surface of the holder, mix your acrylics to get the desired color or consistency (as shown, Katie painted 1 holder all white and another half white). Using a brush (regular or foam), apply the first coat of paint and wait for it to dry before applying a second coat. Paint as many coats as you need until you achieve the desired opacity. Let dry.

3. While waiting for your paint to dry, gather your papers and begin to cut or tear them into various shapes. Start grouping them in interesting combinations, based on similarities and/or contrasts in color, shape, scale, and texture.

> TIP: If any of the papers you want to use have pencil, inkjet ink, linoleum block ink, or any medium that you suspect might bleed when brushed with Mod Podge, test one first. If you find that it does bleed, spray it with a few coats of Krylon Workable Fixatif. Make sure to follow the directions on the can and apply the Fixatif outside or in an extremely well-ventilated area.

4. Loosely arrange your paper pieces on the dry magazine holder so you can see where you might like to place them permanently.

5. Using a foam brush, apply a very thin coat of Mod Podge across the back of 1 of the pieces of paper. Carefully place the paper where you want it on the holder and smooth it out, beginning at the center and working your way toward the edges. If you have a brayer handy, you can roll this over the paper too. With a damp paper towel, wipe away any excess Mod Podge that has seeped out from beneath the paper. Apply the rest of your images in the same way, taking care to apply Mod Podge to the entire backside of each piece. This will help to eliminate subsequent air bubbles when you apply more Mod Podge later.

6. Once all of your papers have been applied, you can choose to simply coat the entire piece with a Krylon UV-Resistant Clear Acrylic Coating or apply several coats of Mod Podge for a more traditionally lacquered découpage look. (Make sure to follow the directions on the can and apply the acrylic coating outside or in an extremely well-ventilated area.) The acrylic coating alone will help to protect the piece from any fading, but the paper pieces might be more susceptible to future wear and tear.

7. If you decide to coat the holder with Mod Podge, apply a thin coat, as you would a coat of paint. Let each coat dry for 30 minutes to 1 hour. If you begin to see air bubbles beneath the paper, don't be alarmed—they will usually smooth out as the Mod Podge coat dries. Apply at least 3 coats of Mod Podge.

TIP: If you do encounter an especially stubborn bubble or wrinkle, it may be because you didn't apply enough Mod Podge to the back of the paper. Carefully prick the bubble with a pin and apply a small amount of Mod Podge through the pinhole with the pin. With your finger, go over the bubble to smooth it down.

8. After you've let the final coat of Mod Podge dry, you can apply a coat or two of the acrylic coating to eliminate tackiness and to further protect the magazine file from the sun and normal wear and tear.

9. Let the magazine holder dry overnight.

KATIE HANBURGER is a graphic designer, maker, and illustrator. She lives in Los Angeles, which is appropriate considering her interest in the intersection of the practical and the imaginary. She has her own studio (Ktothet.com) and is a partner in The Slow Season (Theslowseason .com) with friend and fellow maker Julie Cho.

Chapter 6:
A New Look at Papier-Mâché

Photo of Gemma and her work, circa '60s.

A New Look at Papier-Mâché

Papier-mâché is French for "chewed paper." It's a versatile craft technique that can make use of materials you are likely to already have on hand: newspaper, recycled packaging, glue, twine, paint, and varnish. There are also commercial products available at many craft or art-supply stores that expand the range of possibilities.

The following projects are just a sampling of the many ways to create with papier-mâché. You can choose to cover an existing object, use boxes or wire to shape a new form, or re-create complex shapes using a mold. The basic steps include the application of wet papier-mâché (most often a mixture of glue and water) to form the surface, decoration using paint and other materials, and varnish to seal the surface and maybe give it a little shine.

Many of you will remember doing a papier-mâché project or two when you were young, and you probably haven't thought much about it since. I think papier-mâché has gotten a bad rap. In the popular mind it's often considered cheap, temporary, and theatrical, perhaps best suited for a parade float or theater prop, but there's also a lot of potential in the technique for making really beautiful things. Try it again and I think you might be surprised by the possibilities.

CRAFTY LADY

Gemma Taccogna: Papier-Mâché Extraordinaire

A few years ago, I received a package from a friend in the Midwest who was always finding great stuff at the local estate sales and thrift stores. As I opened the box I saw a few vintage raffia flowers peeking out at me. Of course that made me happy in itself, but it was the vessel for the flowers that really piqued my interest.

It was a little papier-mâché vase with a woman's face painted on it, made in that '60s style that I have always loved—vivid colors, raised textures, and an antiqued finish. I wrote a blog post about it and got a comment telling me the name of the woman who created it: Gemma Taccogna. The more I learned about the work of Gemma, the more intrigued I became. As it turns out, the particular style of papier-mâché that I have always admired, so popular in the '60s, was actually originated by this one very talented woman.

Born in Italy, Gemma was an artist from a very young age. Her family did not believe in giving children toys, so she created her own using flour, paper, and water. In 1937, she ran away from home and settled in Greenwich Village, New York, where she attended Cooper Union. In the '40s she had her first success selling her designs to popular designer Mr. John, who used Gemma's heads to display his hats in his New York boutique. It wasn't long before Neiman Marcus placed an order.

In 1953, she moved to Mexico to start a papier-mâché studio, and she went on to create amazing work that was collected by Peggy Guggenheim. In 1966, Gemma closed her shop, discouraged after seeing her work copied and mass produced by others. She moved back to the United States and continued to create, expanding into other media including tiles. Mary Tyler Moore and other Hollywood celebrities commissioned work from her. She was also a much-loved art instructor.

To this day papier-mâché artists marvel at the smooth, porcelain-like surfaces Gemma was able to achieve in her pieces. Fashion designer Anna Sui has an extensive collection of her work.

Lady Vase

by Katie Steuernagle

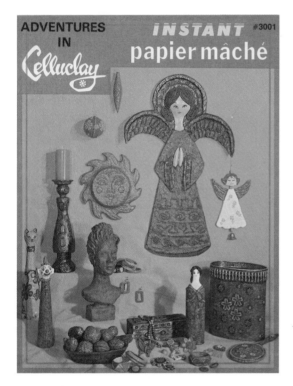

◆◆◆◆◆◆◆◆◆◆◆◆◆◆◆◆◆◆◆◆◆◆◆◆◆◆◆◆◆◆◆◆◆◆◆

I first found out about Katie when I saw her on *The Martha Stewart Show* making cute little papier-mâché squirrel pull-toys. When we talked about the possibility of her creating a project for this book, I introduced her to Gemma's work and encouraged her to do a little research. To say that Katie was profoundly inspired by Gemma would be an understatement. Heavily under Gemma's influence, Katie created this amazing vase. I am sure that Gemma would be proud!

- Large plastic container, for mixing papier-mâché
- Dust mask
- Fine-grit sandpaper (#220)
- Pencil
- Lady Vase templates (see templates)
- Small plastic container, for the glue
- White craft glue
- Soft, fine paintbrush, for details
- Scissors
- Large, soft, flat paintbrushes (for larger areas)

MATERIALS

- Pre-packaged papier-mâché mix such as Activa Fast Mâché (works well because it dries fast) or Activa Celluclay
- 1 empty 2-liter soda bottle
- One 5-in/12.5-cm cardboard circle
- One 8-oz/225-g package Creative Paperclay
- 2 yd/1.8 m 6-ply cotton twine
- Acrylic craft paint (as shown here in beige, light red, dark red, pink, black, white, aqua, and off-white)
- Water-based polyurethane

INSTRUCTIONS

1. Put about 1 cup of dry papier-mâché mix into a plastic container and add water according to the instructions on the package. Mix well.

2. Smooth the papier-mâché in a ½-in-/12-mm-thick layer onto the top third of the soda bottle, leaving a hole about 2 in/5 cm below the bottle opening. Allow it to dry completely.

3. Pop the dried papier-mâché form off the bottle.

4. Make another form exactly like the first.

TIP: Papier-mâché doesn't keep very well after it has been mixed. Only mix what you need and make a fresh batch when you need more later.

5. Join the 2 forms together, small end to small end, and smooth more papier-mâché around the seam where they come together. Allow it to dry.

6. Add a bottom to your vase by cutting a circle of cardboard to the size of the opening (approximately 5 in/12.5 cm), setting your vase on top of it, and smoothing papier-mâché around the seam between the cardboard circle and the vase. Allow it to dry.

7. Add a layer of Paperclay to the vase by pinching off a marble-sized piece and pressing it onto the vase with your fingers. With wet fingertips, spread and smooth it out until it's about ⅛ in/3 mm thick. Add another piece of Paperclay next to the first so that the edges overlap a little to create a continuous smooth layer. Continue adding more Paperclay, wetting your fingertips as you go, and smoothing all the pieces together to create a solid, smooth layer about ⅛ in/3 mm thick around the entire outside of the vase. Allow it to dry completely.

8. Wearing a dust mask to keep from inhaling the dust, sand the surface of the vase with fine sandpaper until it is very smooth.

9. Sketch the trim design (the raised areas around the base and bow detail in front) onto the vase very lightly with a pencil. Use the photo of the finished project as guide for the trim and you may use the template provided for the bow.

10. Using a small bowl, thin 2 tablespoons white craft glue with a 5 or 6 drops of water. Dip about 2 in/5 cm of twine into the glue mixture, lay the end of the twine on your pencil line at the bottom of the vase, and continue pressing the twine down along the line. Add more glue to the twine with a small paintbrush as you go.

Snip the tails of the twine with scissors. Allow the glue to dry completely. For the bow, again dip the end of the remaining twine into the glue and, beginning in the center where the tips of the shapes touch, press the twine along the pencil line. Using the same technique described before, brush glue onto the twine with a small paintbrush as you press the twine around the loops of the bow, painting 1 or 2 coats as needed.

11. Using the beige color, paint the entire vase. Allow it to dry. This acts as your base coat as well as the coloring for the lady's face and neck.

12. Using the template provided and the photo of the finished project as a guide, sketch the face onto the vase. In the lighter red color, paint the lower 1¾ in/4.5 cm of the vase (it will just reach the bottom of the bow), the top 3¼ in/ 8.5 cm of the vase (leaving the face area open), and the interiors of the bow including the twine. Allow it to dry.

13. In the darker red, paint the "apron." Allow it to dry.

14. In pink, using a fine paintbrush, paint the skirt stripes, bottom twine, and the flowers (which you may sketch first using the template provided), on each side and back of the babushka's scarf. (Only 1 of these flowers is visible in the photograph, but with a flower on all 3 sides, this vase is lovely viewed in any direction). Allow it to dry.

15. Using a fine brush, paint the face details (sketch first using the template provided), using black, white, aqua, and pink. Allow it to dry.

16. Paint the interior of the vase off-white. Allow it to dry.

17. Brush 2 coats of polyurethane with a soft flat brush onto the entire exterior and interior of the vase.

◆◆◆◆◆◆◆◆◆◆◆◆◆◆◆◆◆◆◆◆◆◆◆◆◆◆◆◆◆◆◆◆

TIP: This vase is best used for dry flower arrangements. Pouring water in the vase is not recommended!

◆◆◆◆◆◆◆◆◆◆◆◆◆◆◆◆◆◆◆◆◆◆◆◆◆◆◆◆◆◆◆◆

KATIE STEUERNAGLE's first papier-mâché projects were candy-filled piñatas that she made for friends' birthday parties back in the '70s in Dallas, Texas. Today she still loves to hand-craft beautiful and functional objects for everyday living. Katie has appeared on *The Martha Stewart Show* and she loves to share tutorials on her blog, Matsutakeblog.blogspot.com. She currently lives in Minnesota with her family.

Enid Collins at work in her studio, circa '60s.

CRAFTY
LADY

Enid Collins: Made Especially for You

I was browsing eBay one day in search of vintage papier-mâché jewelry, when a big handmade floral brooch caught my eye. It looked like it was made in the late '60s and the back was marked with the initials "ec." The opening bid was very low so thought I might have a good chance of winning, but it was not to be. When it sold for a few hundred dollars, my hunch was confirmed: it was by Enid Collins.

Enid is best known for her celebrated box and bucket handbags, but she also made jewelry and home décor items in papier-mâché. Most crafters I know are influenced by her designs and many of them collect her handbags. Her fans are devoted, and you need look no further than Flickr to see countless images of Enid's work.

I think the level of detail, use of color, and painterly feel of Enid's designs have an appeal to crafters, but it's also her graphically inventive and whimsically named projects, such as "Sophistkit" (cats), "Wise Guy" (owls), "In the Swim" (aquatic life), and "Flutterbye" (butterflies). Some of her other favorite themes included the signs of the zodiac, San Francisco cable cars, peacocks, ladybugs, roadrunners, and her beloved horses. Many of her bags were charmingly inscribed with "Hand Decorated for You" or "Made Especially for You."

After a few years studying fashion design, Enid married sculptor Frederic Collins and moved to a horse ranch outside of Medina, Texas. In the late '50s, Enid and Frederic collaborated on a line of handbags. These first bags were made using fine materials like leather and brass ornaments, which made them very expensive to produce. Enid knew that in order to reach a larger audience she had to bring the production cost down. Her answer was the box bag, made of wood.

Her work began gaining notice and eventually Neiman Marcus placed a big order. As her business grew, Enid employed the wives of local ranchers to help decorate her bags, including the silk screening of the designs. The bags were made in Medina, but her papier-mâché designs were produced by artisans in Puerto Rico. Enid's papier-mâché designs were only manufactured from 1966 to 1968, which makes them very rare and highly sought after by collectors.

Enid enjoyed considerable commercial success during the '60s, but the fact that her work still enjoys a devoted following more than forty years later is an even greater measure of her success.

Antiqued Jewelry Box

by Lara Bobo

Of course my love of Enid Collins made me want to find out more about her. My searches led me to very little biographical information on Enid, let alone any photographs of her. While researching this book, I began to dig a little deeper, and I found that there was a shop in Fredericksburg, Texas, that bore her name. That's how I met Lara Bobo—Enid's granddaughter— and, much to my delight, she had photographs of her grandmother.

I needed to contact Lara one day and had misplaced her contact information so I took another peek at her shop's Web site. I was so excited to find a section on her site with her own jewelry designs! Since she, too, was a designer, it was only natural that I invite her to create a project for this book.

Lara created a jewelry box in the style of her grandmother's papier-mâché work. Her father, also a jewelry designer, also lent a hand, so three generations of talent went into the creation of this project.

The surface of the box is antiqued. Antiquing, a very popular finish in the '70s, involves rubbing a darker color over a lacquered surface and then wiping it down to create a faux "aged" look. My mom's découpage phase happened to coincide with her antiquing phase, and antiqued surfaces figure heavily in my childhood memories of our home's crafty atmosphere.

- Sandpaper, fine (#180–#100) or medium (#80–#60) grit (optional)
- Pencil
- Super Glue
- Elmer's white glue
- Shallow pan
- Masking tape
- Artist's paintbrushes, size of your choice
- Rag (a soft, old T-shirt works well)

MATERIALS

- 1 wooden box (Lara used an old one that her father made, but you can find similar ones at a craft store.)
- 3 round, 19-mm plastic jewels, in gold
- Five 16-mm-x-13-mm teardrop-shaped plastic jewels, in purple (Tip: If you can source vintage glass jewels, they also work very nicely.)
- 2-mm cotton twine
- Water-based primer, in white
- Acrylic craft paints (as shown here in gray, green, pink, purple, orange, metallic gold, and black; Lara used FolkArt brand paints)
- Water-based lacquer spray

INSTRUCTIONS

1. Using the sandpaper, give the box a light sanding as needed.

2. Use a pencil to sketch your design either by following the photo of the completed project or creating a design of your own.

3. Use Super Glue to adhere the jewels to the box according to your design.

4. Measure and cut strips of twine to fit your design. The amount will be determined by your design. Lara used 12 pieces.

5. Mix 1 part white glue and 1 part water in the pan. Soak the strips of twine.

6. Lay the moistened strips of twine along the penciled lines on the box. Allow them to dry.

7. Cover the jewels with a few small pieces of masking tape. This will protect them during the next few steps.

8. Paint the entire box, including the twine, with white primer, taking care not to get paint on the jewels. Allow it to dry.

9. Following the color scheme as shown in the project photo, use acrylics to paint the outside of the box and your design on the box and allow them to dry. You can mix in a little white paint with the colors for the flowers to create a graduated effect as you see in the photo. You may also paint the interior of the box if you wish.

10. Dip the paintbrush in metallic paint, and run it along the edges of the box. A few strokes of gold on the leaves will give it a nice accent too. Allow the paint to dry.

11. Spray the box with 2 coats of lacquer. Follow package directions and use it in a well-ventilated area. Allow it to dry in between coats.

12. Antique the box by dipping a rag in black paint and rubbing it over the entire box. The surface will be slick since the box has been lacquered. Moving in circles, rub the black paint off immediately before it dries. You can use a paintbrush to get in close to the design. The box should be evenly speckled in black with accents around the design.

13. Finish by spraying with as many coats of lacquer as you'd like. Allow it to dry in-between coats. Remove the masking tape from the jewels.

LARA BOBO designs and crafts jewelry from metal, stones, wood, and leather. Though her grandmother Enid Collins passed away when Lara was only five, she left behind a heritage of great style and artistry that continues to shape Lara's work today. Lara lives with her husband, Tim, in Fredericksburg, Texas, where all of her designs are made by hand. Visit her online at Enidlifestyle.com and laracollins.com.

Butterfly Scatter Pins

by Cathy Callahan

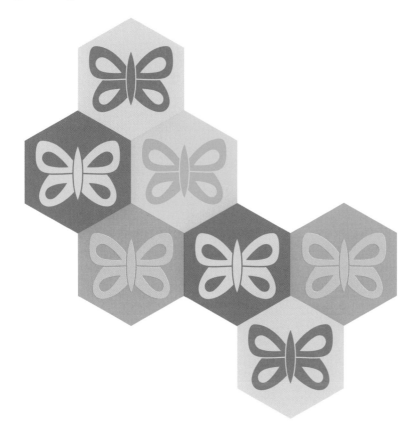

There are some things that I have discovered about vintage crafts that I did not find in the pages of a book or magazine. Sometimes I need to find inspiration by physically holding an object—inspecting it to get a feel for how it was constructed. I eventually did find a couple of Enid Collins papier-mâché brooches on eBay and they are now among my most prized possessions. By studying them carefully, I gained insight into how they were made.

Enid's jewelry was created in much the same style as the other popular papier-mâché of the day, but her signature style of floral, fish, and butterfly shapes set her designs apart. I wanted to make something inspired by her pieces but also add another element, so I decided to also incorporate the fine Belgian linen that Enid used on many of her bags.

- Butterfly Scatter Pins templates (see templates)
- Paper scissors
- Pencil
- Fabric scissors
- One ¾-in-/2-cm-wide sponge brush
- Mod Podge
- Aleene's Tacky Glue
- Tweezers (optional)
- Toothpicks
- Fine artist's paintbrush

MATERIALS (FOR 1 PIN)

- One 8-in/20-cm square thin cardboard (Tip: recycled packaging, such as a cereal box, works well.)
- One 8-in/20-cm square linen or fabric of your choice
- 2 ft/61 cm 20-lb-test natural hemp cord
- Acrylic craft paints in 3 colors (I used FolkArt brand paints.)
- Four 7-mm flat-back round plastic cabochons
- Two 9-mm flat-back round plastic cabochons
- Two 11-mm flat-back round plastic cabochons
- One 1½-in/4-cm pin back

INSTRUCTIONS

1. Using paper scissors, cut out the Butterfly Scatter Pins template pieces, and trace their outlines onto the cardboard. Then cut out the cardboard shapes.

2. Use the cardboard shapes to trace patterns onto the linen. Trace 2 each of the Body and Wings. Make sure to also trace the bottom line of each upper wing (the line intersecting each wing). Using the original pattern to determine placement, trace the Wing Detail (4 times) onto what will be the top set of Wings. Cut out the linen shapes using fabric scissors.

◆◆◆◆◆◆◆◆◆◆◆◆◆◆◆◆◆◆◆◆◆◆◆◆◆◆◆◆◆◆◆◆◆◆◆◆

TIP: Linen can be expensive, but for this project you only need a little bit, so a linen napkin works quite well.

◆◆◆◆◆◆◆◆◆◆◆◆◆◆◆◆◆◆◆◆◆◆◆◆◆◆◆◆◆◆◆◆◆◆◆◆

3. Using the sponge brush, spread an even layer of Mod Podge on both sides of the cardboard Wings and Body. Line up the corresponding pieces of linen, and gently apply them to the cardboard, smoothing out air bubbles with your fingers. Set the Body aside to dry.

4. While the Mod Podge is still wet, the Wings are somewhat pliable. Fold the Wings directly in half down the middle (along the vertical line where the Body will go) and open them back up; they will have a slight V shape. Then gently curve the right and left wings back with your fingers. They will now have a more natural shape. Allow them to completely dry and they will retain this shape.

5. For the antennae, cut two 2½-in/6-cm lengths of hemp cord. Moisten each piece slightly by brushing on a little water and Mod Podge. You will notice that these lengths will have a slight bow to them (i.e., still holding the shape of being on the spool).

6. Run a bead of Tacky glue down the middle of the front of the Wings (in the "fold" you made in step 4).

Lay 1 of the lengths of hemp down, making sure that the bottom edges are flush and that a little more than 1 in/2.5 cm of the hemp extends from the top. Repeat with the other length of twine.

The pieces of hemp that stick out over the top of the wing section become the "antennae." While the antennae are still moist, shape them so that they fan slightly away from each other.

7. For the outline of the Wings, cut two 4-in/10-cm and two 3-in/7.5-cm lengths of hemp cord. Moisten each piece slightly by brushing on a little water and Mod Podge.

8. Run a fine bead of glue along the edges of the Wings, including that section that intersects each wing. Place the longer lengths of hemp all the way around the tops of the Wings, including the intersections, and the smaller lengths around the lower Wings. Snip off any excess. Tweezers might help you with this step. While the glue is still wet, adjust the position of the hemp to make clean crisp lines. Clean up any excess glue with a toothpick. Allow the glue to dry.

9. Apply another layer of glue down the middle of the Wings and lay the Body section on top of the twine used for antennae. Refer to the finished project photo for exact placement. Allow it to dry.

10. Using acrylics, paint the Wing Details on the Wings, and allow the paint to dry. Do 2 coats if necessary.

11. Glue the cabochons in place (follow placement as shown in the photo of completed project) and allow them to dry. Paint the stones with 2 to 3 coats of acrylics.

TIP: The painting for steps 11 and 12 requires a steady hand. You may also choose to paint the stones and/or cord prior to gluing them down.

TIP: I painted the stones so that they matched my color scheme. You may choose to leave them unpainted or substitute rhinestones or other gems of your choice.

12. Using the fine paintbrush, paint the outline and antennae cords. Allow them to dry.

13. Run a bead of craft glue down the back center of the pin-back and apply it to the back of the butterfly, making sure the clasp is at the bottom. Allow the glue to dry.

To Wrap It Up . . .

While I was working on this book, my boyfriend had a very interesting observation. He thought that the way the contributors approached their projects was not unlike the way musicians cover songs for those tribute albums that are collections devoted to one particular band, singer, or composer—typically someone of note who continues to inspire and entertain new generations of fans. The artists who record songs for these albums take the spirit of the original, but give it their own personal stamp, all while paying high honor to the original artist. I think that the same level of admiration and respect was used in every project in this book. Ultimately, this book pays tribute to all of the creators of the crafts from the '60s and '70s.

Throughout this process, I was fascinated and impressed by the ideas that the contributors conjured up—ways to make these projects truly their own. They took approaches that I never would have thought of had I done the projects myself. I have a feeling that if you, too, start to explore the amazing pages of craft books and magazines from the '60s and '70s, you'll discover a wealth of inspiration for exciting new ideas of your own. The possibilities are endless.

Resources

EBAY.COM
For all things vintage craft-related, from how-to books to supplies. Also great deals on new supplies.

ALEENE'S TACKY GLUE
Available at most craft stores.
Manufactured by I Love to Create.
Ilovetocreate.com

BURLAP
Used in projects in Chapter 1 (page 10)
Purchased at Michael Levine:
920 Maple St.
Los Angeles, CA 90015
Mlfabric.com

A smaller range of colors is also available at: JoAnn Fabric and Craft Stores
Joann.com

STYROFOAM SHAPES
Used in Mushroom Pincushion (page 15)
Purchased at Michael's:
Locations throughout the United States
Michaels.com

Also available online from:
Save-on-crafts.com

TRIM
Used in Mushroom Pincushion (page 15)
Purchased at M & J Trimming:
1008 Sixth Avenue
New York, NY 1001
Mjtrim.com

MOD PODGE
Available at most craft stores.
Manufactured by Plaid.
Plaidonline.com

SOBO PREMIUM CRAFT AND FABRIC GLUE
Available at craft and fabric stores.
Manufactured by Delta Creative.
Deltacreative.com

CRAFT PAINT
Many projects in this book use FolkArt Acrylic Colors. They are inexpensive, have very good coverage, and are available in dozens of colors. Available at most craft stores.
Manufactured by Plaid.
Plaidonline.com

RAFFIA
Used in the Wall Hanging (page 35)
Purchased from Raffit Ribbons:
Raffit.com

HANA-AMI FLOWER LOOM
Used in the making of the Wall Hanging (page 35)
Available at Michael's and Jo Ann's.
Manufactured by Clover.
Clover-usa.com

GALLERY PANEL/ ART BOARD
Used in Wall Hanging (page 35) and String Art (page 77) projects
Purchased at Blick Art Materials:
Dickblick.com

JAPANESE SASHIKO THREAD & NEEDLE
Used in Wall Hanging (page 35)
Purchased from Purl Soho:
Purlsoho.com

VINTAGE SWISTRAW
Used in Place Mat Project (page 37)
Purchased on eBay.

HEATH CERAMICS VASES
Used in Free-Form Crochet Vase Covers project (page 43)
Heathceramics.com

ERICA WILSON'S (PRO- FILED ON PAGE 53) NEEDLEWORK KITS
Available from Erica Wilson Needleworks:
25 Main St.
Nantucket, MA 02554
508-228-9881
Ericawilson.com

EMBROIDERY SUPPLIES AND CARBON TRANSFER PAPER
Used for Embroidered Snail Pillow (page 67)
Purchased from Sublime Stitching:
Sublimestitching.com

WOOL FELT
Used for Embroidered Snail Pillow (page 67)
Purchased from Giant Dwarf:
Giantdwarf.etsy.com

FLOWER POTS
Used in Macramé Hanger Project (page 73)
Available from EcoForms:
Ecoforms.com

EPHREM'S BOTTLE CUTTER KIT
Used in Bottle Wind Chime Project (page 83)
Available from art and stained-glass suppliers. Also readily available on eBay.

GLASS PAINT: LIQUITEX "GLOSSIES" HIGH-GLOSS ACRYLIC ENAMEL
Used in Bottle Wind Chime Project (page 83)
Purchased at Blick Art Materials:
Dickblick.com

MAGAZINE FILES
Used in Découpage project (page 105)
IKEA'S "KNUFF"unfinished birch plywood magazine holder
IKEA.com

ACTIVA FAST MÂCHÉ OR ACTIVE CELLUCLAY
Used in Papier-Mâché Vase Project (page 105)
Available at most art-supply stores.
Manufactured by Activa Products.
Activaproducts.com

CREATIVE PAPERCLAY
Used in Papier-Mâché Vase Project (page 113)
Available at most art-supply stores.
Manufactured by Creative Paperclay.
Paperclay.com

PLASTIC JEWELS
Used in Antiqued Jewelry Box Project (page 117)
Purchased from Plastic Beads Wholesale:
Plasticbeadswholesale.com

Acknowledgments

This book would not have been possible without the friendship, support, advice, and handholding that I received along the way. My most heartfelt thanks and everlasting appreciation goes out to the following:

My contributors—Susan, Jenny, Kayte, Diane, Cecily, Laura, Erika, Hannah, Nicole, Cathy P., Derek, Lauren, Robert, Billie, Tootie, Jill, Lucy, Katie H., Tom, Susie, Heidi, Meg, Katie S., and Lara. Each and every one of you exceeded what was asked of you and created some truly beautiful craft projects.

The team at Chronicle Books—Christina Loff, Jodi Warshaw, Aya Akazawa, Emily Craig, Molly Jones, and—most of all—Laura Lee Mattingly. Thanks for believing in me and giving me the opportunity to do this book.

Meiko Takechi Arquillos for taking such exquisite photographs of the projects and her super talented assistant Simone Lueck.

Alexis Hartman for her expertise in illustrating the project diagrams as well as some of the patterns and templates.

At the heart of this book are the images from vintage craft magazines and books. The expert guidance of the extraordinary Piper Serverance is what made the arduous task of tracking down the copyright holders possible.

My deepest appreciation goes out to everyone who kindly granted me permission to use their copyrighted material (as well as those who provided invaluable information that helped guide me in my search) especially Tiffany Windsor, Vivian at Meredith Corporation, Charles Phoenix, Carl W. Griffith, Erica Wilson, Jean Ray Laury, Roz Dace, Allyson Dias from I Love to Create, Kasey Jones from Plaid, Genell from Activa, Gemma Del Rio, and Lara Bobo.

To all of the authors, designers, art directors, photographers, and stylists who worked on my beloved craft books and magazines from the '60s and '70s: Many of them were uncredited and I hope that in some way this book pays honor to your hard work.

To all of the "hoarders" who saved their books, magazines, craft supplies and objects from the '60s and '70s that have since made their way to eBay and thrift stores so that we may continue to use and enjoy them.

To the faithful readers of my blog—thanks for liking what I do.

And most of all, thanks to my wonderful boyfriend Scott for everything and for serving as my "in house" design and editorial consultant on this book.

Photo Credits

Image on page 6
Cover of *Dip Film Flowers,*
Copyright © James E. Gick
1968. Courtesy of the
Gick Family.

Image on page 9
Photo of Aleene Jackson
from *A Tacky Lady* by Aleene
Jackson, 1997. Courtesy of
Tiffany Windsor on behalf
of Aleene Jackson Museum/
Inspired at Home.

Image on page 12
Cover of *Make It with . . .
Yarn 'n Burlap* (Hazel Pearson/
Craft Course Publishers, Inc.,
1969). Courtesy of Tiffany
Windsor on behalf of Hazel
Pearson Archives.

Image on page 13
Photo of Hazel Pearson from
A Tacky Lady by Aleene
Jackson, 1997. Courtesy of
Tiffany Windsor on behalf
of Aleene Jackson Museum/
Inspired at Home.

Image on page 15
Mushroom Pin Cushion
from *Burlap Bounty* (Hazel
Pearson/Craft Course
Publishers, Inc., 1967).
Courtesy of Tiffany Windsor
on behalf of Hazel Pearson
Archives.

Image on page 23
Plastic Bottle Birdhouses
from *McCall's Needlework &
Crafts* Spring-Summer 1964.
Used with permission from
Meredith Corporation. All
rights reserved.

Image on page 27
From the *Vintage Slide
Collection of Charles Phoenix.*
Courtesy of Charles Phoenix.

Image on page 33
Cover of *Swistraw and Flower
Looms* by LeJeune Whitney,
1972. Copyright © LeJeune
Whitney images. Courtesy of
Carl W. Griffith.

Image on page 35
2 Crafty Ladies from *Ribbon
Straw—An International
Handicraft (*Hazel Pearson
Handicraft, 1967). Courtesy of
Tiffany Windsor on behalf of
Hazel Pearson Archives.

Image on page 39
Cover of *Serendipity in
HiStraw.* Copyright © 1970
Columbia-Minerva
Corporation.

Image on page 43
Free-Form Crochet from
Crocheting with Swistraw
by LeJeune Whitney, 1972.
Copyright © LeJeune Whitney
images. Courtesy of Carl W.
Griffith.

Image on page 47
Crochet Wall Panel from
*McCall's Annual of Creative
Handcrafts Vol. 1,* 1969.
Used with permission from
Meredith Corporation. All
rights reserved.

Image on page 52
"Dendriform" Wall Hanging
by Jean Ray Laury. Courtesy of
Jean Ray Laury.

Image on page 55
Re-embroidered fabric
designed and worked by Erica
Wilson on Vladimir Kagan
chair from *Needleplay* by
Erica Wilson, 1972. Photo-
graph courtesy of Erica
Wilson. Photograph by
Michael Tcherevkoff.
Erica Wilson Needleworks
25 Main St.
Nantucket, MA 02554
508-228-9881
Ericawilson.com

Image on page 59
Aprons from *Better Homes
and Gardens Gifts to Make
Yourself,* 1972. Used with
permission from Meredith
Corporation. All rights
reserved.

Image on page 63
Felt Fruit Projects from
*McCall's Needlework &
Crafts* Spring-Summer 1970.
Used with permission from
Meredith Corporation. All
rights reserved. Photo by
William Benedict.

Image on page 72
Macramé and String Art
from *How to Make Plant
Hangers* by Lynn Paulin, 1974.
Copyright © James E. Gick,
1974. Courtesy of the
Gick Family.

Image on page 81
Painted Stones from *The
Beautiful Crafts Book,* 1976.
Photograph copyright ©
Search Press Ltd.

Image on page 83
Wind Chimes from *Bottle
Cutting and Decoration*
(Hazel Pearson/Craft Course
Publishers, Inc., 1972).
Courtesy of Tiffany Windsor
on behalf of Hazel Pearson
Archives.

Image on page 87
Cover of *Projects Made of
Folded Magazines, A Craft
"How-To" Create Book* by
Aleene, 1966.
Copyright © I Love To
Create, A Duncan Enterprises
Company.

Image on page 92
Cover of *Rags to Riches with
Mod Podge* by Jan Meyerson
Wetstone. Photo used
with permission from Plaid
Enterprises.

Image on page 95
Closet holds Gift Wraps from
*Better Homes and Gardens
Christmas Ideas* 1965. Used
with permission from
Meredith Corporation. All
rights reserved. Photo by
Hoebermann Studio.

Image on page 99
"New Tissue Paper Painting"
from *McCall's Needlework &
Crafts* Spring-Summer 1961.
Used with permission from
Meredith Corporation. All
rights reserved.

Image on page 101
Stationery from *McCall's
Needlework & Crafts* Fall-
Winter 1971–72. Used with
permission from Meredith
Corporation. All rights
reserved.

Image on page 105
Cover of *The Craft of
Decoupage* by Patricia
Nimocks, 1972. Photo used
with permission from Plaid
Enterprises.

Image on page 110
Photo of Gemma Taccogna
from *Papier-Mâché Artistry*
by Dona Z. Meilach, 1971.
Photograph courtesy of
Gemma Del Rio. Photograph
by Jim Schumacher.

Image on page 113
Cover of *Adventures in
Celluclay,* 1967. Images and
photographs courtesy of
Activa Products.

Image on page 116
Enid Collins in her studio.
Courtesy of the Collins Family.

Most photographs are repro-
duced courtesy of the creators
and lenders of the material
depicted. For certain artwork
and documentary photo-
graphs, we have been unable
to trace copyright holders. The
publishers would appreciate
notification of additional credits
for acknowledgment in future
editions.

Index

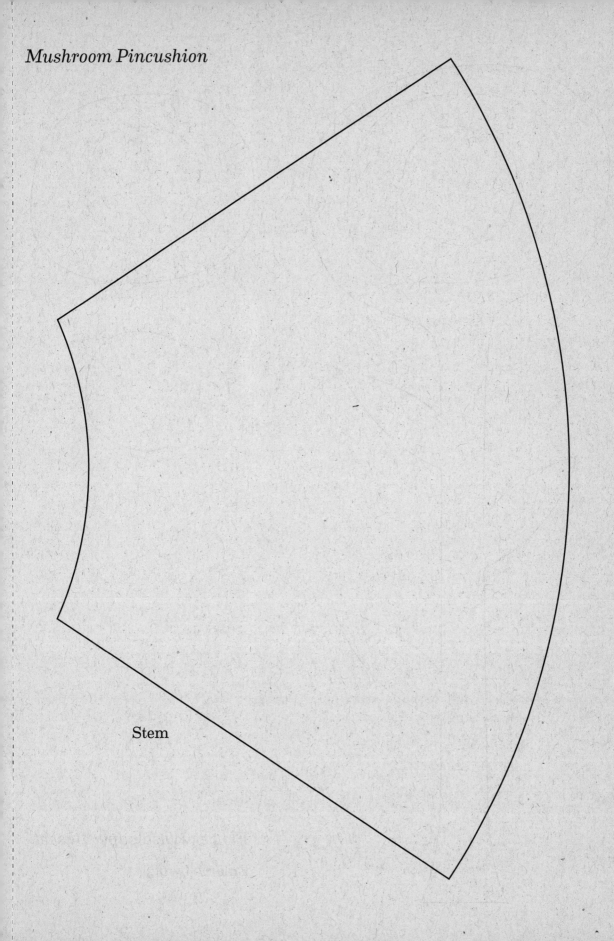

Mushroom Pincushion

Stem

Flower Wastepaper Basket

Enlarge by 143%

Body

Underside

Gone Fishing Tote

Bag Top

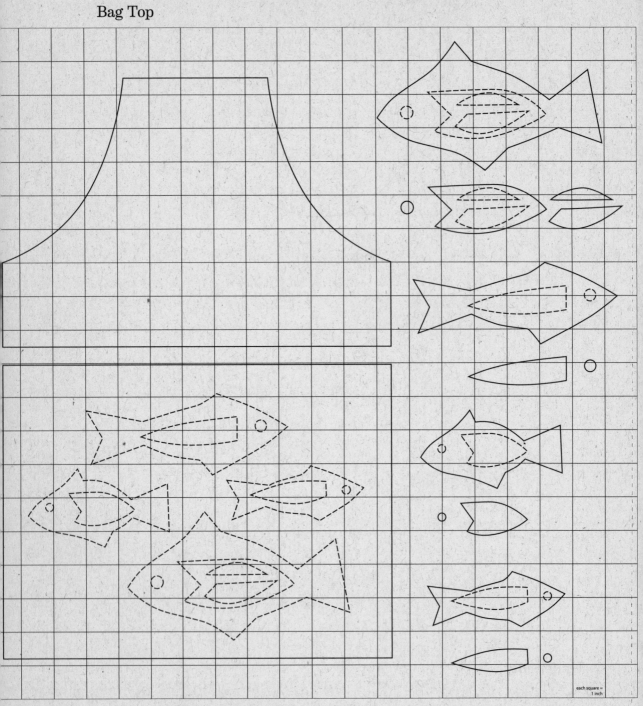

Bag Bottom

Enlarge by 286%
(Each square should be 1 in/2.5 cm)

Tulip Apron

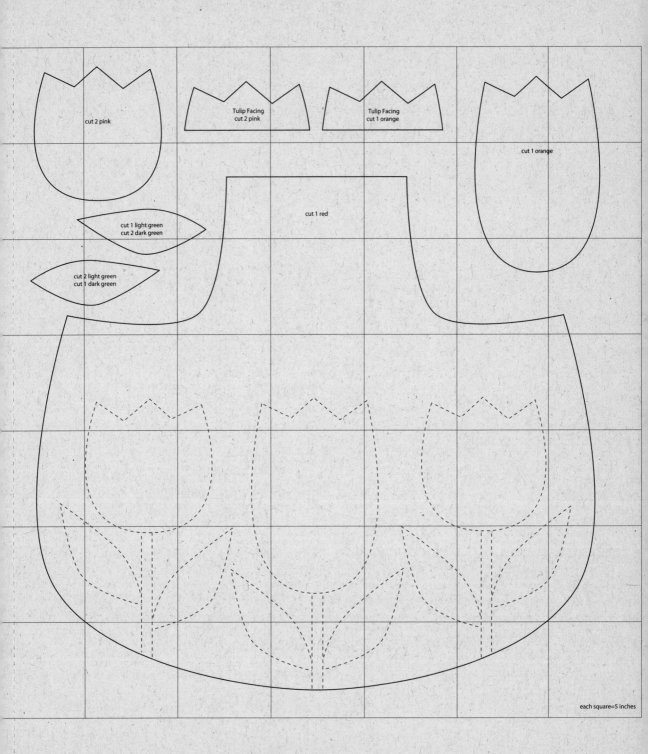

cut 2 pink

Tulip Facing
cut 2 pink

Tulip Facing
cut 1 orange

cut 1 orange

cut 1 red

cut 1 light green
cut 2 dark green

cut 2 light green
cut 1 dark green

each square=5 inches

Enlarge by 500%
(Each square should be 5 in/12.7 cm)

Embroidered Snail Pillow

Enlarge by 167%

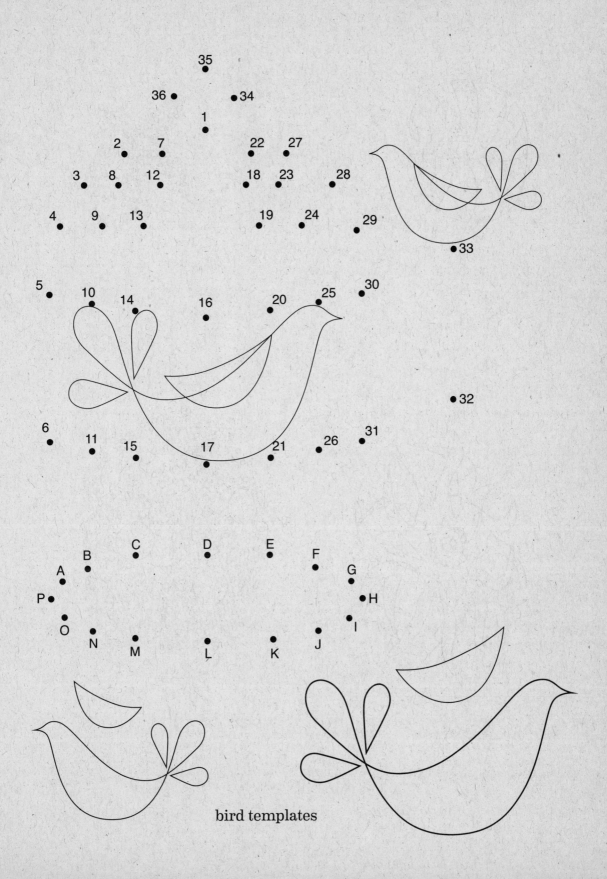

bird templates

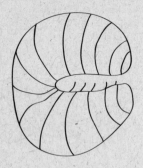

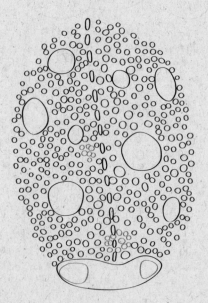

Festive Gift Boxes

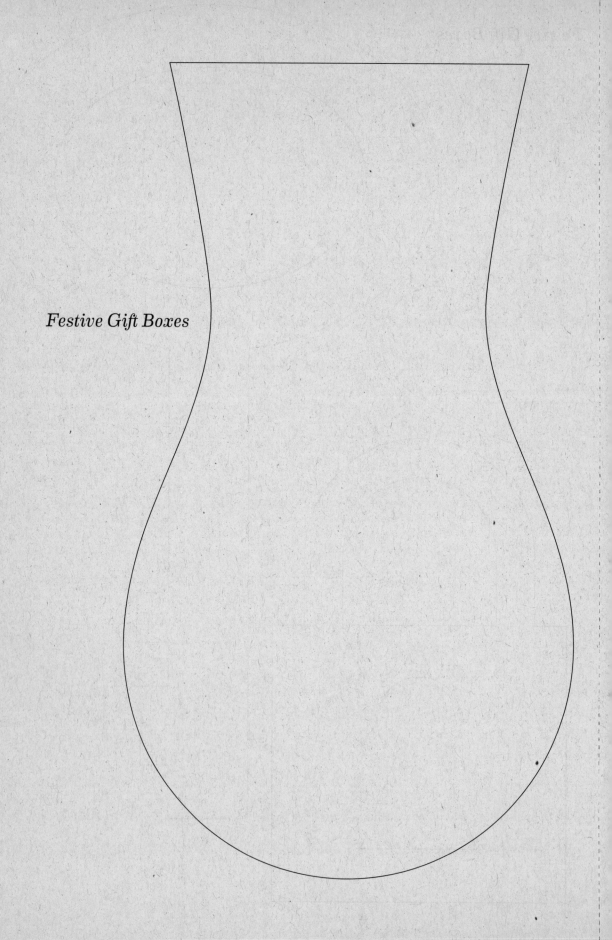

Festive Gift Boxes

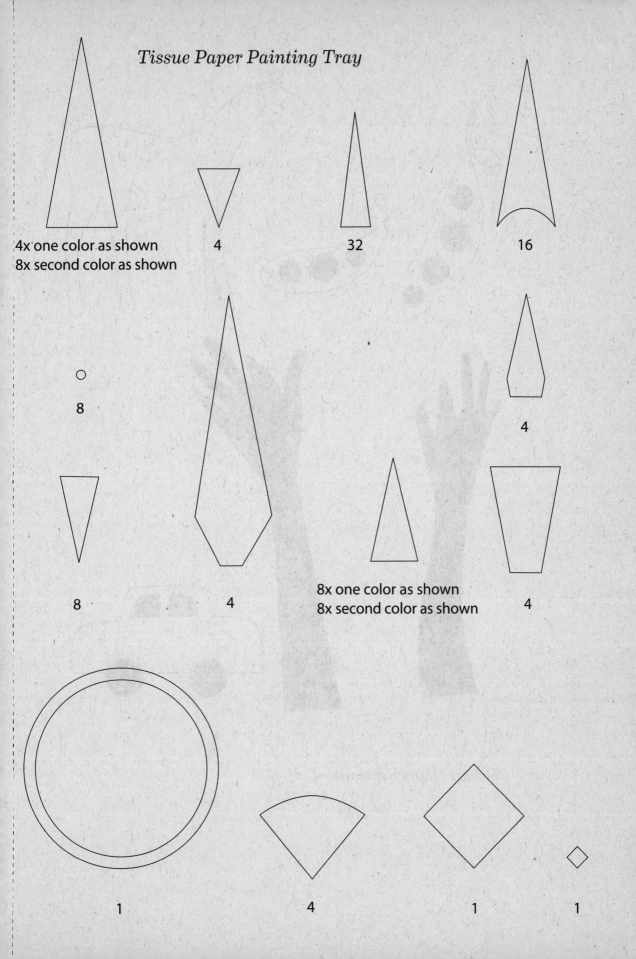

Tissue Paper Painting Tray

4x one color as shown
8x second color as shown

4

32

16

8

8

4

8x one color as shown
8x second color as shown

4

4

1

4

1

1

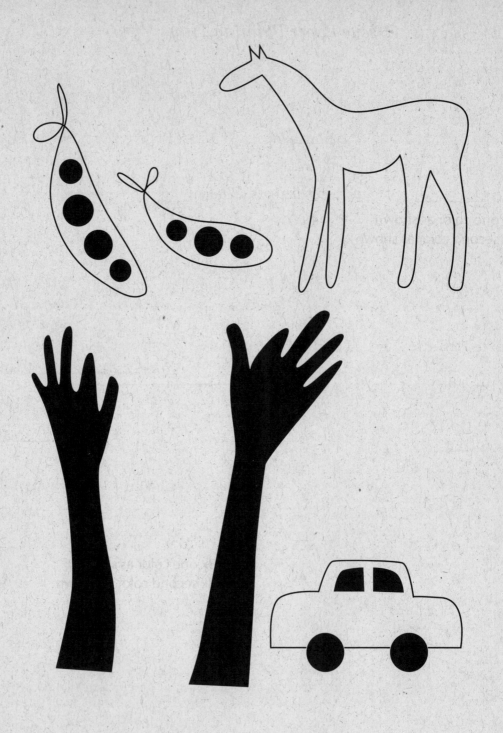

Scrap Notes Stationery

Lady Vase

Butterfly Scatter Pins

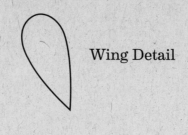

Wing Detail

Body

Wings

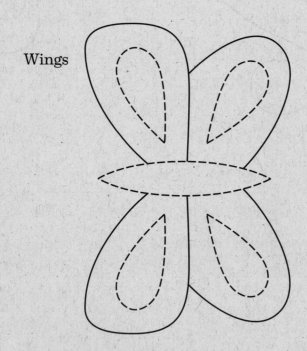